Praise for *Smal...*

"Ballard lays out so much information [...] we have read about and never got the real lowdown on how to actually do. ... This is a book you need to read."

—Tish Owen, author of *Spell It Correctly*

"Ballard has given us what we've craved for decades: a down-to-earth, easy-to-read instruction manual filled with practical magical solutions, all of which can be performed with items you already have on hand.

—Dorothy Morrison, author of *Everyday Magic*,
The Craft, and *Utterly Wicked*

"Each chapter [is] filled with truth, common sense, practicality, and uncomplicated lessons in the learning and unlearning of being magical beings."

—Angie Buchanan, senior minister of Earth Traditions
and founder of the Death Midwife

"Byron challenges us to recognize and harness the power of simplicity and small magics. ... She cuts to the chase regarding the misconceptions and history of witches and magic and offers real-world practical steps."

—Patricia Ballentine, priestess and creatrix of the
Temple of the Creative Flame

"What you'll find within these pages is common-sense folk wisdom, remedies, and practices ... and a welcome perspective that the magical world all around is not only accessible to us, it is also part of us."

—Miles Batty, author of *Teaching Witchcraft*

"It has the no-fluff, to-the-point, do-the-work kind of stuff that you will want to refer back to time and time again. It is absolutely chock full of those nuggets of wisdom practice."

—Sam "Bo" Thompson, author of *Metal Never Lies*

"Byron has a beautiful, non-judgmental cadence to her writing that helps the reader understand concepts that many in our work complicate with esoteric high witchcraft language. Byron brings truth to the table."

—Tanja Bara, elemental natural magick and
Hoodoo practitioner, teacher at Tanja's Natural Magick

"Ballard writes about magics in a clear and kind voice. … Her work gives you options, a place to start, and ways to think about your practice that are invaluable."

—Christine Cunningham Ashworth,
author of *Scott Cunningham: The Path Taken*

"Ballard encourages us to notice and appreciate the primal energy sources that are everywhere in nature and in ourselves, and she teaches us how to tap into our own power and confidence by using simple and effective methods."

—Denise Alvarado, author of *Witch Queens, Voodoo Spirits, and Hoodoo Saints* and *The Magic of Marie Laveau*

"With her customary wit, warmth, and candor, Ballard … deftly lays out a clear and central witchcraft practice without pretense that anyone from any region may find a home in."

—Tara-Love Maguire, coauthor of *Besom, Stang, and Sword*

"An indispensable opportunity to walk alongside the village witch herself as she shows us what it takes for us to run."

—Christopher Orapello, artist, cohost of *Down at the Crossroads* (podcast), and coauthor of *Besom, Stang, and Sword*

"*Small Magics* lays out the essentials of magic for the new practitioner with Ballard's trademark practical wisdom and humor while offering the more experienced witch useful reminders and creative inspiration. ... Ballard also points to the future of magic, encouraging us to take our enchantments out into our communities."

—Diotima Mantineia, creator of Urania's Well and author of *Kiss the Earth, Touch the Sky*

"*Small Magics* is that tool you've longed for since you first heard the word *magic*. ... Held within these pages is a wealth of simple and straightforward suggestions for both beginner and adept on how to make your work even more effective and pleasurable."

—Arlene Bailey, author and artist, creator of the Facebook page The Sacred Wild, Re-Membering the Wild Soul Woman

"A practical, how-to manual ... that will guide you step by step through the basics of spellwork. ... Ballard gifts the reader with useful magic, sound ethics, and timeless psychological advice."

—Ellen Evert Hopman, author of *The Sacred Herbs of Samhain*

"Whether you are new to witchcraft or just want to see things from the perspective of a folk magic witch, this will be a great addition to your witchy bookshelves."

—Roxanne Rhoads, author of *Haunted Flint*, council chair for the Michigan Black Hat Society, and high council member of the National Black Hat Society

Small Magics

About the Author

H. Byron Ballard, BA, MFA, is a western North Carolina native, teacher, folklorist, and writer. She has served as a featured speaker and teacher at Sacred Space Conference, Pagan Spirit Gathering, Southeast Wise Women's Herbal Conference, Glastonbury Goddess Conference, Heartland, Sirius Rising, Starwood, the Scottish Pagan Federation Conference, HexFest, and other festivals and conferences. She is a cofounder of Asheville's Coalition of Earth Religions (CERES) and Mother Grove Goddess Temple, where she serves as senior priestess. She podcasts about Appalachian folkways on *Wyrd Mountain Gals*.

Her essays are featured in several anthologies, and she writes a regular column for *SageWoman* magazine. Her books include *Staubs and Ditchwater* (2012), the companion volume *Asfidity and Mad-Stones* (2015), *Embracing Willendorf* (2017), *Earth Works: Ceremonies in Tower Time* (2018), *Roots, Branches & Spirits: The Folkways & Witchery of Appalachia* (Llewellyn, 2021), and *Seasons of a Magical Life: A Pagan Path of Living* (Weiser, 2021). She is currently at work on a book on the divine feminine, a cookbook, and a musical adaptation of Shakespeare's A *Midsummer Night's Dream*. Visit www .myvillagewitch.com.

Small Magics

Practical Secrets from an Appalachian Village Witch

H. Byron
BALLARD

Author of *Roots, Branches & Spirits*

Llewellyn Publications
Woodbury, Minnesota

FIRST EDITION
First Printing, 2023

Cover design by Shannon McKuhen
Cover illustration by Jerry Hoare / Donna Rosen Artist Representative
Interior art element by the Llewellyn Art Department

Photography is used for illustrative purposes only. The persons depicted may not endorse or represent the book's subject.

Llewellyn Publications is a registered trademark of Llewellyn Worldwide Ltd.

Library of Congress Cataloging-in-Publication Data (Pending)
ISBN: 978-0-7387-7370-4

Llewellyn Worldwide Ltd. does not participate in, endorse, or have any authority or responsibility concerning private business transactions between our authors and the public.

All mail addressed to the author is forwarded but the publisher cannot, unless specifically instructed by the author, give out an address or phone number.

Any internet references contained in this work are current at publication time, but the publisher cannot guarantee that a specific location will continue to be maintained. Please refer to the publisher's website for links to authors' websites and other sources.

Llewellyn Publications
A Division of Llewellyn Worldwide Ltd.
2143 Wooddale Drive
Woodbury, MN 55125-2989
www.llewellyn.com

Printed in the United States of America

Also by H. Byron Ballard

Staubs and Ditchwater
(Smith Bridge Press, 2012)

Asfidity and Mad-Stones
(Smith Bridge Press, 2015)

*Embracing Willendorf: A Witch's Way of
Loving Your Body to Health & Fitness*
(Smith Bridge Press, 2017)

Earth Works: Ceremonies in Tower Time
(Smith Bridge Press, 2018)

Roots, Branches & Spirits
(Llewellyn, 2021)

Seasons of a Magical Life: A Pagan Path of Living
(Weiser, 2021)

Dedication

There are women, past and present, who practice the most profound and authentic magic but cannot, for myriad reasons, call themselves *witch*. They are following the work of previous generations as they tend to and reweave their communities with all the skills they own. We owe them more than we can ever repay. This book is for them. We stand together shoulder to shoulder, hip to hip, and calf to wheel.

Contents

Acknowledgments

Books don't write themselves, you know. In addition to the haggard author, there is always an indispensable and ragtag army that brings tea, ignores the mess, and exclaims over the smallest success. That army, for me, consists of Joe, Kat, Jeff, and the ever-hungry Pepper Jack; my Patreon supporters (whom I refer to as my Matreons); the Mother Grove Goddess Temple Circle of Council and the wonderful volunteers who keep the home fires burning in my absence; and the vast, beautiful community that has formed on Facebook. My editor (and friend) Heather Greene, Lauryn Heineman, Shannon McKuhen, Donna Burch-Brown, and the rest of the team at Llewellyn take thousands of words and transform them into a real, live book and have my gratitude and respect. I asked several friends who wear prosthetic devices, notably Angie and Monica, if I could hear more about the intricacies of their magical practice, and they graciously responded. Barb, Al, and Friends at the Farm gave me space, time, and quiet to work on edits. All these beings are golden. If there is any confusion or any inadequacies, they are mine and mine alone.

Introduction

Amidwinter storm blew in this morning before the sun had risen enough to light the snow. Wind and bits of ice struck the front window, and I woke to the swaying shadows of the witch hazel that guards the walk to the porch. Under my quilt and flannel sheets, I thought through the day that had come and set some intentions to focus my mind (and to enjoy the coziness a little longer). Then I rose and made my bed, steeped a cuppa tea, and sat down to write a book for you—a book about the whys and wherefores of having a simple and helpful magical practice.

Why would I do such a thing when there are so many magic books on the market in this heyday of witchcraft? Why am I writing another book? I am the village witch of this place, and I teach magical practice at festivals and conferences. *Village witch* is an old descriptor for a person, almost always a woman, who serves her community with advice and traditional herbal medicine, who attends births, deaths, and everything in between. My village began as my local community, where I do all the above as well as clearing energy in homes, businesses, and houses of worship and sometimes speaking to the media. Now my village has stretched through social media and festival travel to a much broader village, as I share community building and Appalachian folk magic: an old folkway that I advocate for and happily practice. My world is imbued with love for the woven basket of my community and a deep concern for the natural world. That is more than enough to fill my sweet life.

Lately, in teaching and doing workshops, I begin each class by thanking the people who invited me—to dance with them what brung me, to paraphrase the late Molly Ivins—and acknowledging the ancestors and spirits of the land. Then I continue with a solemn plea to those people in the group who consider themselves magic-workers of some sort. I explain a bit about these challenging years in which we live. I call this Tower Time, and I implore the group to practice their Craft until they are not merely competent but adept. I tell them that the earth needs them, that their species needs them, that their communities need them. Please, oh please! Practice magic and energy harvesting and management until you are really, really good at it. Don't save it for a rainy day because the sky has been overcast for a good long time and the rain is already pelting down.

Does this little drama work? Do some of those people do what I ask of them? Yes, they do. Or at least they report to me that they are working hard and practicing. I am taking them at their word. As we delve deeper into these challenging, Tower-falling times, one of the drumbeats that pulses through my days is the need to prepare ourselves and our communities for the days that lie ahead.

When I began teaching these crafts, I soon discovered that the majority of students and seekers had never had access to a live teacher. They had learned what they knew about these practices by reading books (many of which offer contradictory ideas) or through asking other relatively new practitioners for help via social media. What they almost never have been taught are the very basics of magical practice: how to ground themselves, to shield themselves and ward their environs, to gather energy from the natural world and utilize it, and to set clear intentions.

Out of this need, I developed a class called "Simple Practical Magic," and after a few offerings, I began to invite seasoned practitioners to sit in—not because they didn't know these techniques but because I had found it personally helpful to regain my "beginner's mind." I was able to refresh details that I found I was glossing over in my own practice. I personally love to sit in on beginner classes to see how other people achieve the things I do. It's instructive, it's fun, and it satisfies my curiosity to explore new protocols and to support my friends and colleagues in their work. This led to wonderful discussions and a belief that knowing the basics—and learning to walk before you try to run—is terribly important but often skipped for the more dramatic parts of being a magic-worker.

This book is an introduction to the ways of magic as practiced by a folk magician and an experienced witch. I will share the basics and explain some definitions that maybe we can agree on. What is magic? Why do it? How do you do it? Can anyone do it? The book includes those building blocks of magical practice and details techniques for grounding, relaxation, breathing, and accessing available energy. Protocols for shielding and warding are presented with an admonition on the importance of practice. This is not a spiritual book—though there is some discussion of engaging noncorporeal beings (including ancestors) as allies in the work.

Learning the mechanics of this kind of energy work is often a case of cobbling together things we've read, experiences we've had, and stories we've heard. There is little hands-on training available to many people, and this book on the basics of magical practice from the experience of a seasoned witch may be helpful.

Let me be very clear on this point: this is not the only way to practice magic, and these are not the only techniques. This is how I do it, and my hope is that you will test-drive the practicum parts and see if they work for you, that you will tweak them if they aren't right for you and go on to create your own techniques. Ultimately, I want you to have the experience and the courage to teach what you know and start the whole process again with the next generation, whatever their age, of magic-workers. Some of the material here has been reverse engineered—I did a thing and was successful in doing it but didn't know the actual steps to the process. I worked on it again and again until I knew what I had done and why it achieved the desired results.

Here I am at the start of a new book on old ways of doing and of being. The sun is well up now and I've stepped out onto the porch to release any residual anxieties of the day and concern about my ability to do this project. I pull into my hands the brisk, clear intention of a January wind on its way to the other side of the country, and, unburdened by doubt, washed clean, my hands are ready to do the work of my head and my heart. I finished some writing and unwove some of my thoughts.

And so it begins, the spiral of learning, unlearning, and relearning. I know you're ready and willing, curious to know what you may not know and looking forward to having the right tools to live a full, magical life in our deliciously magical world.

Chapter 1
To Do the Work

I often write from the perspective of my cultural folkways. Most people think of me as an Appalachian witch. But I learned over many years of face-to-face teaching with generous and competent teachers, information from books, and good old trial-and-error that there are techniques that are used across cultures and economic classes and techniques that are both old and new. There are as many techniques as there are definitions of magic, and this diversity gives us strength and resilience, especially when we can compare notes with other practitioners, something I will always recommend. We are in a time—mostly through the fear that is generated in social media—when sharing can bring both critique and mockery. If you truly desire to walk this road—if you are called to these winding paths—you will do well to let that go and do your work, do the Work. You are not competing with anyone except yourself, and your goal is to become an adept, someone who knows magic well and uses it effectively.

Magic-Worker and Witches

Throughout this book, I will use the phrase *magic-worker* to denote a person who uses magic. There are plenty of words for such a practitioner and many of them are very loaded, especially if we are working outside our personal cultural milieu or working with others who don't share a common language with us. I use the word *witch* in many places but not all. In my native culture in the southern highlands, traditional folks can be leery or frightened of that word, and Cherokee, African American, and Mexican friends have a very different and potentially threatening definition of that word—a word that people of European descent have reclaimed from our witch-hunting and witch-obsessed history. Be sensitive to the uses of language and try not to be stubborn and "right" about it if you want to have real conversations about this energy work with authentic practitioners outside the narrow bounds of your personal experience. That's good manners, and those, as well as a genuine curiosity, will get you farther than you might think, even in our modern and argumentative world.

During my years as a playwright, I wrote a play called *The Burning Times: A Study of the Continuing Inquisition*. It is a two-act exploration of the witch trials in early modern Europe and how they have influenced Western culture down to the present day. Many of us, especially politicians who regularly use the phrase *witch hunt* to describe the media investigating their shenanigans and malfeasance, have the mistaken idea that these horrific things only happened in the distant past. But witch hunting and murder is still a global phenomenon. The word *witch* is one I happily reclaim because of this significant period of our collective history. But not all do and not all can. It is important for us to remember that as we stretch the web of our work throughout the worldwide web.

Abolish "Mundania"

The world—the earth and its beings—is an inherently magic-filled place, enchanted and inspirited. It is our birthright to practice the magic that is so abundant, that has been entrusted to us by the land with which we dwell, by our ancestors and by our teachers (whether corporeal or not). It is a gift that should be handled with care and received with gratitude. Try to remember those bits too, in among the curiosity and courage, the good manners and the practice. To live a life in which you practice energy work also gives you some obligations to manage, some expectations to temper.

Our entertainment is rife with magic and the people and things that wield it. Myths, books, and films can inspire us to amazing heights while also giving a false idea of what magic looks like when it does work. It is often less about fireworks and more about deep satisfaction for achieving a difficult thing. Most often, it is about making your life a little easier because you can efficiently find a parking space in a busy urban area or relieve yourself of the fears and anxieties that hold you back from achieving bigger goals. Big and little magics—they are all welcome and all possible, and matching the working to the goal is something we all learn with experience.

I've written elsewhere about the need to open our eyes to the inherent magic of the world. I'm an animist. I see the world as inspirited, that everything in it has a soul and is inherently alive. It's an old-fashioned worldview that seems to have been with me when I was a child, and the sense of and belief in that spirit world has never left me. When people leave a festival or other gathering with others of like mind, there is a collective sigh about returning to "Mundania," where no one will understand them and they must cloak their true selves in the garb of the uninitiated and uncool.

Stop it.

You don't need to walk through your town in a long black cloak wearing a pentacle the size of a salad plate to show you're a witch. You certainly can do that if you choose, if it makes you feel grand, but it's hardly necessary. The people who need to know you will know what and who you are.

There is some discussion in social media about the world being more magical than it has been, more haunted, more visited by beings from across "the veil." This is not true. We are simply more aware of it than we used to be, and it has become socially acceptable to speak in those terms. The world does not need us to "re-enchant" it—it needs for us to pay attention. And as we wander these paths, I will ask you again and again—are you paying attention? Magical practice is most deeply and easily grasped when we observe the world around us, both the seen and the sensed. We must deeply engage all the senses available to us to understand and to absorb their meaning and instruction. We would do well to simply pay attention and to listen.

What Is Magic?

Greater minds than mine have answered this question again and again. There are always tweaks and additions, and as you grow your practice and enhance your ability, you will have your own definition, one that fits your view of life, the universe, and everything.

A possible working definition is this: magic is a set of skills and abilities with which the practitioner changes the world around them through the deft use of the energies available to them, the intentional modification of the culture and world we inhabit.

Let's look at that and break it down.

"Skills" refer to the techniques you learn and master in the practice of magic. "Abilities" are not only those learned skills, but also what you bring to the work through your life experiences and gifts. In my part of the world, there is a surprising number of people who have precognition in one form or another. Many rarely use it or even acknowledge it—it's good for a funny story at a party or a family tale about your peculiar great-aunt. And in many places in the world there are extraordinarily sensitive people who seem to feel all the emotions of the people around them, for good or ill. There are other examples of gifts that seem to come to us without any prompting, which is why they are called gifts. All gifts can be strengthened through practice and can be understood better when we converse with others who seem to have the same gifts. We will look at this is more detail—and with an Appalachian flavor—in chapter 4.

When we desire to change the world around us—find a new job, get into a training program, grow a bountiful garden—we can bring the intentional and energetic part of our practice to the physical, day-to-day part. As we interweave our lives with this energy work, we engage in a hands-on and tangible way as well as a magical one. Both/and, belt and suspenders, holistic. There is no need to fragment our lives and our world into separate parts when we can braid them together to be more effective and more satisfying.

The deft and effective use of energy is what this book is all about. Keeping your work efficient as well as skillful will allow you more time and mental space to do the work as it comes to your hand. As you simplify your magic, you will be quite likely to simplify your life too. There is so much beautiful work to do in our engaged and flourishing lives.

For me, the truest definition is this: magic is that thing that both is and operates the universe.

Sphincter Magic

This phrase always gets a laugh when I teach, but I'm afraid it is a visual joke. When most of us start playing around with magic—something I encourage you to do, frankly—we tend to scrunch everything up. We dig our toes into the floor and lock our knees. Then we pull our elbows into the sides of our bodies, making hard little fists with our hands. We tighten all our muscles (including the ones in our bottoms) and we hold our breath, grunting with the effort of "making magic." Anyone observing this display could easily push us over onto the floor like a statue from a plinth.

I call this "sphincter magic" and I don't want you to do that anymore. The practice that I use and teach is the polar opposite—an opening to and harvesting of the energies all around us. Relax.

I don't care what your sartorial style is—enjoy it in whatever way makes you feel frolicsome and do it *for you* because you want to and it pleases you, not because some talking head demanded you conform. But you don't have to dress any particular way to announce your status as a magic-worker. The way people will know who and what you are is by your deft practice of these techniques and by your confidence and kindness in the world. You do not need to wear that jumbo-sized pentacle to announce your presence to the world. Enough people will be clamoring for your attention and your help without hanging out a shingle on your chest.

The actual practice of magic requires a relaxed but focused approach. If you tighten your entire body and try to squeeze out enough energy to do the work, you will have cut off the flow of energetic input from the world around you. You reinvent yourself as an island of pretend power, easily flustered, easily toppled.

When you tighten up your core from the outside in, you cut off the paths by which energy moves from the earth and the sky and you force your body to use its natural energy, your life force. With continued magic in this style, you end up diminished and tired and your magic is simply not as effective, and it is certainly not as easy. I have found no advantage to making work harder—any kind of work. There is no virtue is working harder than is necessary to achieve a task, no matter what John Calvin thought. When a job of work is presented to you, it is best to go through your personal discernment process, get the job done, and have a cuppa tea. Unless the work requires a theatrical touch, you are wasting precious time showing others how fancy your magic looks, instead of simply doing the energy work required for the task at hand. This isn't stage magic. It's manipulation of energy to a desired end.

In chapters 5 and 6, we will look at some helpful techniques for relaxing our bodies into the work at hand. We'll see how that difference feels (physically and emotionally) and how it affects the success rate of our work.

Why Do Magic?

Is that an actual question? Most cultures on the planet are filled with stories of magical occurrences facilitated by magical beings. Magic is the weird sticky substance that attaches our dreams to our daily lives. Magic is power for the powerless, justice for the oppressed, the sense of agency that a dominating culture simply will not grant us.

Magic, dear reader, is power.

Imagine for a moment the meeting room in a public library, reserved by a librarian for a "women's discussion group." The facilitators have brought cushions and pillows for the floor, and a plastic table holds stacks of mismatched cups and thermoses of herbal tea. There are candles carefully enclosed for safety but there is no incense. The meeting begins with "housekeeping": welcoming those assembled, pointing out the bathrooms, reminding the women that they have to be out by 8 p.m. The subject tonight is self-reflection as a prelude to self-empowerment. Many words and much tea later, the group plans to meet again and, individually, the women feel seen and heard. They feel stronger and they wonder what it means to hold this amorphous thing called power.

Fast-forward to today, when we still grapple with power—not the holding of it but the wielding of it. Many of us, especially women, have spent decades sitting in circles, working on empowerment. With perseverance and a good deal of luck, some of us came out of those mostly navel-gazing experiences ready to take action to heal the world and our immediate community. We were empowered to do so—like getting a hall pass or permission slip. Then we stood in our power to model strength and resilience for those who sought it.

It is time for the next step, the place where most of us are now as we contemplate the uses of power. There is much to be said for author Riane Eisler's *The Chalice and the Blade*, a book that introduced many of us to the difference between *power over* (the dominator model with which we are most familiar) and *power with* (a sharing of power and authority as well as a restructuring of standard concepts of leadership).

When we are open to the idea that power can be shared, we may choose to step into a share of that power. As you've read these words, there have probably been other examples that have come to mind. When we begin with why practicing magic is important in our day-to-day lives, we quickly see the possibilities of creating change around us. We can begin to consider how much agency we can have in the workings of the culture.

The techniques and protocols outlined in this book are mostly the result of me learning this craft over decades, screwing some things up, figuring out what did and did not work and applying that information to make my work more effective and efficient. So much of what we do as magical practitioners is the result of trial and error, which I have found is one of the best ways to learn anything.

I have been a student of languages since my Lutheran kindergarten teacher taught us some German. Wending my way through Latin, French, more German, Gaeilge, and now Italian, I am not fluent in any except my native language. I am merely functional in the others. I suspect the best way for me to gain fluency is a full immersion program where I am forced to speak and to understand in order to eat and find a place to sleep.

It is the same with magic. We can read many books and watch hours of video, but until we muster the courage to do it, we won't become the adepts our communities need. Sometimes it requires an emergency to push our baby-bird selves out of our nest of books and prove we can fly.

When we return to our simple definition of magic as the intentional modification of the culture and world we inhabit, it's easy to stop there without thinking about what that kind of modification requires of us as the modifiers. The work of magic can take a toll on the practitioner. If we are not accustomed to preparing ourselves for the work, we can neglect the helpful warm-ups that ensure right practice. When that happens, it makes sense to stop and step back into beginner's mind. It is a concept from Buddhism that invites us to reframe our experience and to start again with fresh eyes and curiosity, as a beginner in any field often does. Taking it step by step—relax, ground, harvest energy, focus, and then pick up your pre-crash intention—lets us see what part we were leaving out, the bit that made the entire working unbalanced and lacking.

In those times of unbalance, we may forge ahead without the necessary reevaluation. It is then we may find segments of our lived experience dropping away or rearing up in our faces to get our attention. Let those not-so-subtle signs serve as a reminder to stop and evaluate before the red flags accumulate and effectively block your practice and sour your joy.

We will revisit this idea from time to time in the following chapters, but best to start as we mean to go on. Don't use magic as the last resort in a difficulty. Instead of exhausting all other options and then asking all your friends to light a candle for you, have enough magic at your fingertips to start there and then add on to it. You just got a pink slip and the job market in your field is tight? Do magic … and then clean up your résumé, activate your networks, tighten your belt, and do all the other things. Magic is another tool in your tool kit, and if you keep it sharp and well-oiled, its use will facilitate the movement you require in a given situation.

But it won't work as well, if at all, if the first thing you do is put "a spell for finding a job" in a search engine and then wade through all the ads and garbage that will undoubtedly come up first. Once you have mastered the techniques and protocols outlined in this book, you'll have a good idea of how to proceed in most situations. Knowing those things will also give you the confidence to do your very best and then judge the results.

Why do we do magic? We do magic to change what needs to be changed to make the world healthier and more just. We do magic to connect us to the deep workings of the world and the universe in which it nests. We do magic because we are healers, exploring the Great Mysteries.

And we do magic because it is fun.

⤛⤜

NOW YOU TRY

Throughout this book, I'll do a brief summation of the chapter, then invite you to try something or think about the material in the chapter. You may choose to journal about the experience or your thoughts, either on paper or electronically. Either way, I do highly recommend that you spend at least a few moments closely considering the contents of each chapter and how the ideas affect your own practice. Review your journal entry to see if you find this new information helpful, then add your personal adaptations.

This chapter is about the beauty of simplifying your magical practice, making time in your day-to-day world for intentional energy work, and employing the idea of beginner's mind as you test your skills.

What could you do with unlimited time to explore, to practice, even to play with magic? How does your definition of magic differ from the ones in the chapter? Is your spellwork more complicated than it needs to be? Try simplifying one of your usual workings and see if it still does the job.

Hint: To change your thinking about magic, try setting aside the preconceptions of magic and its practice that you learned from TV and movies. Start fresh.

Chapter 2
That's Why It's Called "Practicing" Witchcraft

I harp on this endlessly and am grateful to have the opportunity to write an entire chapter about it. Practice in any field may not make you perfect, but it will make you pretty darned good. Practice is a commitment to the craft you claim to serve, a commitment that requires you to work at something in order to be good at it.

Practice is a verb and a noun. As a verb it means to rehearse, to repeat something over and over so that when you execute the thing you are practicing, you can expect some degree of success. When we're learning something new, we usually go slowly and repeat what we learn until we have confidence in the level of our knowledge. Once we are fairly solid on the basics, things tend to go faster and our knowledge base grows, allowing us to begin integrating subtleties. In some instances, we pick up the basics quickly and easily but begin to slow down as we incorporate the details of the practice. These are two ways to work and there are many ways to learn—visual, aural, experiential, and more.

When *practice* is used as a noun—when someone asks you about your magical practice—it implies all that the verb brings to the word and makes it personal. Practice implies something you do regularly, a series of exercises that you implement to achieve the desired result. Doctors talk about their practice, and *practice* becomes another word for your business and your work.

Far too many of us, whether we are beginners or experienced, don't practice enough. *Enough* is a relative term, of course, and in this case *enough* means that when called upon, we can perform reasonably well. Performers of all sorts understand the value of doing more than a few minutes every other week. If they make their living performing, they will probably choose to work every day, and if they are in love with what they do, they can't wait to work on that new piece, to write that new poem that is rattling around inside their head, to sing scales for the sheer joy it gives them to make those gorgeous sounds.

Practice makes competence, if not exactly perfection. But practice can be hard to schedule in our busy lives. My fiddle has been in its case for several months now because I see the case, consider opening it, and then get bogged down in thinking ahead to tightening the bow and tuning. My head rejects the embarrassment of hairs exploding off the bow and the way my fingers are going to hurt because I've let them go soft again.

Making Time

Applying your desire to be good at energy work to a vital and interesting practice will require great commitment on your part, but it also requires you to go beyond the commitment to the action and to take responsibility for both learning the techniques and making them your own through repetition. Fortunately, there are ways to hold yourself accountable.

If you are a scheduling sort of person, you can designate a time dedicated to it. Thursday evenings are when the rest of your household is focused on other things and the house is quiet. You usually use that time to catch up on laundry or watch something you like on one screen or another. Instead, you can choose to use all or part of that ninety-minute block to get in some exercise in an area where you feel weak. Half an hour once a week doesn't sound like much, but it can make all the difference in your ability and your confidence. It is "me time" of the best kind. And if we think of it as a special treat that we so richly deserve, it can change our outlook for the better. We can spend time ahead of that brief half hour deciding what we'll explore, making a cup of delicious tea, and "indulging" ourselves in exercising our magic muscles.

You can ask a friend to be your accountability partner, and you can either practice together or hold each other to account for different activities. Your friend needs a little push to get her fiddle out and practice, and you want to get better at grounding. It's most fun if you can set aside the same ninety-minute block and have a conversation immediately after to crow about how excellent you are. But you can have that same conversation at the end of the week in which you both face your practice demons and pat each other on the back. This works so well with exercise, smoking cessation, or modifying other unhealthy habits. It works equally well when you know you want to run through an energy exercise but keep finding excuses not to do it. In this time of challenge, disease, and hardship, it is an act of self-care to carve out time for yourself. Carve out some time for this and it will pay off almost immediately.

Another way you can choose to practice is by grabbing bits of time all day long. I'm a big proponent of using the time otherwise lost at traffic lights while driving to and fro. There are days when I feel like I'm on the road all day long. I tend to gang up errands into one day, so I don't break up each day with a trip out. This wasn't possible when my daughter was in school, and I cherish the long days of gardening, writing, and canning when I can settle in at home for a day of work.

While waiting at a traffic light or in a traffic jam, remember the protocols you are training yourself in and try them out. Shielding practice is easy while waiting, and it's one of the things we need to master. Pull energy into your center from that muffler-deficient car to your right. Prepare a glamour to use on the clerk at the drugstore so that the experience is memorable for both of you—be a rock star who shares her magnetism with the kid who's working at their first real job selling lottery tickets and cigarettes.

See? Magic can be fun and can make the world better as you trail clouds of magic through your daily life, the invisible glitter of goodwill.

Create Space

Once you've figured out making time to practice, you may want to create a space to practice. We all know people who have enough space and privacy to set aside a ritual room. The best I can manage is part of my dining room, a place that isn't used for dining on a regular basis. I also do much of my work outside in the yard or garden. My kitchen table is also utilized for many things besides a bowl of oatmeal in the morning. Many of my online classes and rituals are set up on my kitchen table, after I've cleared the table and washed the supper dishes. The dining room area holds my altars so any work I feel needs to happen at an altar goes there, with the wooden door closed firmly behind me.

The idea of an altar is an interesting one. Many modern Pagans, if they are theists, will have one or more altars around their home or garden. It can be anything from a windowsill to a tabletop to a specially designed piece of furniture. It can be a semipermanent installation that stays in place all the time, perhaps changing as the seasons change. Or it can be portable and live most of its time in a stout box, only to be assembled when needed or desired.

There are altars dedicated to spiritual beings that are used as part of our religious efforts. There are also working altars where our tools are close at hand, and we give ourselves enough space in which to do the work we have chosen to do.

In many parts of the ancient world, altars were often places of animal sacrifice: those heavy old altars from the classical world often feature a channel to drain away blood, a liquid with immense magical power. The sacrifice of animals was a large part of ancient religion as well as ancient magic. There are religious groups today that do the same, so this ancient practice is very much a living one.

For most of us, however, sacrifice becomes metaphorical, symbolic. We sacrifice our egos, our precious time, our prejudices, and many other things that we willingly give up in order to be a better religionist, a better human, a better witch. Our altars, if we have them, tend to reflect that idea of sacrifice and will hold objects that inspire us in our quest for this sort of betterment.

The practices of magic don't usually require a dedicated work area—though that can be very convenient. I find that a supporting but comfortable chair is all I need in the way of dedicated space because I need to do my work in such a way that my body is alert but comfortable. You will find what works best for you—keep trying things and places until it feels right. And I need privacy, of course, so that I am not distracted or interrupted in my work.

Make It Fun

If we treat practicing as a chore that must be done, it becomes oner-
ous. Practice then becomes the grueling steps one must take to do
the "fun" parts of magic. When we reframe that thought—when
practice itself becomes the fun thing—it makes a huge change in
how much and how quickly we learn things. Going into learning
a technique because someone has told you how important it is can
result in a resentment that is not conducive to learning.

Choose some practice pants or a shirt that you love to wear.
We have clothes for riding, yoga, workouts—why not magic practice? Yoga clothes are a good choice because they allow you to
move, aren't bulky, and are comfortable to wear. There is a popular wellness technique called Nia or NIA, which stands for neu-
romuscular integrative action. Like much in American consumer
culture, there soon developed a clothing style for Nia that was
practical enough for yoga or dance but added a flowing outer garment. Many witches are people who are sensitive to the way things
feel as they move through space, and you may find that Nia-style
clothes give you the right sense of movement as you practice.
Since the trend has diminished somewhat from when it was first
launched, these garments are often available in thrift and consign-
ment stores.

Do you need music to set the stage for your work? Do it. Create
a playlist for your practice—mood music to relax and focus you.
My preference is often soothing classical music: Bach, Schumann,
and Debussy are favorites. But when I need an extra boost, I turn
to traditional Irish music and grab something from the Chieftains
or Flogging Molly. We create playlists not only for fun but also
to put us in the right headspace for the chosen activity. You will
know what works for you, and you can change it depending on the

current technique. Grounding may require a different mood than shielding does. Protection magic requires one thing, fertility/creativity magic another.

"Smells and bells" is the humorous description of ritual in some high-church Christian congregations and can also describe some Pagan rituals as well. If you find scents particularly evocative—and most of us do—choose one to add to your practice time, using oils, incense, herbs, or whatever scent brings you into the best connection with the techniques you are learning. My preference depends on the season. I burn dried herbs such as mugwort, rabbit tobacco, or mountain mint in the colder months. I also like sandalwood incense because it reminds me of my grandmother. You may find yourself drawn to lavender, basil, or rich, moist soil.

Lighting may also be important to you. Candles are traditional, but a room softly lit by a lamp in the corner may be more to your liking. You may want a strong desk lamp to cast good light on your work area while the rest of the room is dark. Working by moonlight is also a possibility unless you have fiddly detail bits that you can't quite see. The lighting you choose can determine the level of both focus and sensitivity.

It sounds like a lot of preparation and, of course, you need none at all. You may only want music or scent or, like me, comfy pants. But when we are dodging practice (for whatever reasons), making practice a pleasure and an adventure works to inspire us to put in the work to achieve competence. Getting the space ready is a matter of moments once you've decided. Put on your comfy pants, turn on the lamp, light a candle and incense, turn off the overhead light, play the music—takes three minutes. (I just did it and timed it.) Three minutes to set the stage and get you in the right frame of mind.

You might also consider putting in five or ten minutes of spontaneous practice instead of scheduling a specific time and creating all this folderol. Five minutes when you have them—waiting on the kettle to boil, in line at the store, at red lights on the road, and so on. It helps, just like with exercise. It is better to put in a little time when you can than to wait until you can set aside a half hour and then never do it.

Time

Ideally, how long and how often should we practice?

That is impossible to answer in a general way, and like most everything you'll read in these pages, you will be the one who knows your life, your schedule, and your temperament. We set the earlier example for once a week, but that won't be practical for many. Once you start sneaking in little practice sessions here and there, that may feel like enough. The proof of the pudding, as the old truism goes, is in the eating. Are you better at grounding than you were before you added a practice session every Sunday afternoon? If the answer is yes, and that schedule works for you, the pudding is good. If you are still slow and uncertain about the technique, you may need more frequent sessions that only last for five minutes, or you may need to find a technique that suits you better. If you brush your teeth twice a day, spend one of those brushings practicing a technique. That is often how I work out new techniques—I let my mind wander while I spend the requisite time scrubbing away.

As with everything in this book, I encourage you to keep trying variations until you find the ones that work for you. Magic and magical practice are not one-size-fits-all, and your inspired curiosity will lead you to what you need, as well as what fits in your life.

You may have a well-tuned inner clock that can be very helpful in the practice of magic. Are you one of those people who often know what time it is without looking at a clock? When you aren't bound by someone else's schedule, do you find yourself getting sleepy and waking up at about the same time every day? Time is a strange thing, and I suspect it is something we barely understand. Those of you who are sensitive to time may find it best to have less structured time for your practice and to do it when the hour feels ripe. You may be feeling the influence of moon, sun, and other influences (including your mood) and how well you've been sleeping and attending to your self-care.

Practicing beyond Technique

We've looked at the importance of practicing the stepping stones of magic. You may wonder when you have practiced enough to try some actual workings. That will depend on your level of self-assurance about your progress. I encourage you to always try out some workings when you feel inclined to do it. This doesn't mean you drop your regular practice and focus only on these individual workings. Practice is still important to keep your skills sharp.

When you begin exploring individual workings, as opposed to general techniques, you will probably only perform them as needed. Weather work demands our attention when our needs are not reflected in the natural world around us. Garden is drying out—practice your weather work. Outdoor wedding in your rainy season—practice your weather work. Your auntie is ill and has asked you for prayer and healing thoughts—practice your healing strategy. Healing, though, is one of the few workings that can be practiced at any time so that you are ready when your auntie needs you. There is always someone somewhere who could use extra support through this energy protocol. Possibly it is you yourself who can most benefit from your healing work.

Reverse Engineering

The workings throughout this book have been practiced for many years and are pared down to their bare essence when I do them. For the purpose of the class that this book is based on—and to work with the occasional student—I have to perform the working as I usually do it and check the results. Then it is often necessary for me to reverse engineer what I did to get that result. That is why I am so insistent on you learning the basics, the important building stones of a strong practice. If you skip necessary steps in the interest of time or out of boredom or laziness, you won't be as confident or as effective as I know you can be. My reverse engineering has made me realize how vital it is to be able to shield effectively and quickly, how to ground yourself and reweave your soul and body into a cohesive unit, and the ways in which we can bring needed energy into our center and utilize it in the work of magic. Otherwise I would have been confused about how to teach these simple but important techniques. I took apart the workings in order to see both the ingredients and the techniques and share them with you.

Muscle Memory

I have been focusing on the need to repeat what you learn in order to set it. In movement, we say we move the lessons into *muscle memory*—that is when a habit is so ingrained that you have embodied it. Magic is never a matter of pointing a crooked stick and muttering garbled Latin. The intricate balance of energy in, energy held, intention clarified, and energy out is one that can be learned and then perfected as best we can. It is the difference between a ten-minute guided meditation before you have your shields up and the immediacy of sensing the world around you and protecting yourself immediately, without even thinking about it. Find something you need and do it again and again, until it is firmly in your magical muscle memory. Here's an example that makes sense to most people: if you live in an area with a distinct lack of public parking, create a working that will achieve parking when you need it.

Many of the techniques in this book require practice. When I schedule a practice session for myself—and I do that more often than you might think—I always start with something I already do well. Success first thing is always cheering. I find that I look forward to doing the things I'm confident about. Then I move on to the areas where I need more help. You may choose to dedicate your time to a new skill or trying out a new technique because you like a challenge or want to attain a level of competence to further your other work as a witch and a magic-worker. Practice may not make perfect and that isn't the goal. Practice will make us efficient in the use of resources and effective in the way we move energy. Practice makes excellence.

NOW YOU TRY

This chapter is about finding your personal comfort zone for your workspace, adding small touches that set the stage for your practice, and accepting that repetition is essential.

Finding the best way to practice for your lifestyle and time limitations goes a long way toward setting yourself up for success. Play around with short, medium, and long practice sessions. What have you found is best for you? And do you actually do it?

Try sketching out your practice either in words or pictures to see where the glitches are and how to amend your protocol to really serve you and your work.

> Hint: If you are struggling with establishing a regular practice, try wearing different clothes, changing the smells and sounds around you so that they put you in the magic mood.

Chapter 3
Tools and Definitions

Advanced practitioners usually find that they use fewer and fewer tools as their abilities strengthen. If you have watched the series of movies that features children learning the arts of wizardry and witchery in a magical academy, you'll understand that the beginners learned all the rules and all the words and gestures for success at magic-wielding. If the incantation was spoken in an incorrectly garbled way, dread events might be expected. As the books and films—and the children's schooling—continue, we are allowed to see how the grown-ups do magic. Few spoken words, no careful positioning of wands. To watch the adepts battle each other is a marvel: swifter than the best tennis game and far more deadly. Appear. Strike. Disappear. Reappear. Strike.

We start with the tools we read about in books or that our colleagues recommend. We practice with them and, if they are suited to us, come to depend on them as we do workings. We forget a step one day or accidentally leave our ritual dagger at a friend's house, and much to our surprise, we realize that a pointed finger drew as well as the knife. The next time we may choose to simply use the tool we always have with us—our pointy finger.

I'll give you an example from my spellcasting life. I'll use an egg binding to look at some ways we simplify our use of tools and materials once we've gotten the hang of gathering in energy and sending it out with intention.

An egg binding is a low-level bane that is designed to modify someone else's behavior. This is my technique as I teach it: begin, as in most things, by grounding yourself and setting a clear intention. Using a raw egg (chicken, duck, or whatever you have readily available) and a soft pencil, you write the name of the subject all over the shell, repeating the intention either aloud or to yourself. When the egg is completely covered with writing, check your grounding. It is easy to lose focus on grounding as you are working. Feeling the strength beneath your feet and the energy flowing from the planet to you can mean the difference between success and failure.

Take up a length of yarn—my preference is black or red—and wrap the egg (repeating the intention almost like a chant) until the egg is covered in yarn. The resulting object will be round, rather than football shaped. Place the egg in your freezer for a moon cycle. After that time, remove the object and either bury it off your land or throw it into swiftly running water. Observe the behavior of the subject to see if your working has been effective.

It is generally effective, and I often recommend it because it is simple, is focused, and usually works. As you use this technique, you'll develop shortcuts: you won't cover the egg entirely with either writing or yarn. You will set your intention and get grounded faster, and you won't need to wrap-and-chant, gathering in the necessary energy. You may hold the egg in your nondominant hand and wrap it in red tissue paper.

After years of experience, this is now how I do a binding: I simply press my heels down to ground myself. I extend my nondominant hand palm up and then tap the center of that palm with a finger from my other hand while visualizing the subject. Next, I make a fist with the nondominant hand. And the binding is complete. It takes about ten seconds. It is as effective as the more complicated egg binding. But the reason it works and the reason I can use that technique is because I learned to walk—to do the steps that set up success—before I decided to run. Learning any magical technique and practicing all the steps will lead you to a place of competence that you can't shortcut your way to achieving. It's about practicing the grounding, intention setting, energy gathering, and projection necessary and then executing the working. The final step is to observe and document—to check your math.

This chapter is about all the tools you may need to be effective or that you may want because they are cool. But I want to be clear that these are, for the most part, training wheels on your bike. Pretty soon you'll be able to peddle steadily and not fall over. Pretty soon you'll advance to a bigger bike. But until then, keep your training wheels on because they will build your confidence and ability level.

Getting Started with Tools

Walk into any well-stocked metaphysical shop and you will find tools for every possible magical adventure. Shelves are stocked with nearly every possible divination tool from cards to pendulums and beyond. Candles in every color and color combination invite our scrutiny, and those shops always smell of strong herbs as well as incense. There are rows of shining chalices and inside a glass counter there are athames and bolines with tooled-leather sheaths. It is a smorgasbord of delight and our fingers itch to have one of each, please.

I began with my grandmother's wood-handled steel knife as my ritual knife, and I have it still, using it when necessary. She was a good cook and taught me much of what I know about both cooking and healing. She had her favorite kitchen tools, and this is a knife she didn't use often, an Old Hickory butcher knife. I asked her if I could have it and she assumed I wanted my own special knife for chopping vegetables. I did use it like that for as long as I lived with her, and when I left home, it went with me. I wrapped the handle in leather to make it easier to pull out of the cardboard scabbard I made for it. The cardboard scabbard is likewise covered in soft suede and there are lapis beads sewn onto it. The whole thing fits on a strip of rawhide that ties at the waist. It is as effective an athame as any of the subsequent ones that were given to me as gifts, although those have been lovely too. I'm terribly fond of the one my friend Bill made me from a railroad spike. Twisted and sharp, it would serve me well in a street fight too, I suspect.

When I am in need of a wand, I usually go out to the woods behind the house and see what has been left for me. Not because I don't have a wand—I have a dozen or more—but because my preference is otherwise. I rarely use wands, but people who know me know my love of trees and of fine woods. A local wand-maker had created a wand made of the taproot of a large poison ivy vine and I got to test-drive it. He had coated the dangerous wood so that it was safe to handle bare-handed. It felt amazing, that wand, especially for banework.

My forgemaster buddy created a marvelous wand for me in his magic backyard forge. Blacksmiths are awfully magical folks and always have been. A forge—even the portable ones that sometimes appear at summer festivals—is a place of deep and dangerous transformative power. Places of power should be honored as such, and weaving a relationship with both the place and the keeper of the place is a wise decision. I keep that fire-and-iron wand in a safe place near my home altar, and the honor bestowed on me by its creation, its creator, and its gift still strike at the core of my heart.

Some tools you will encounter or that will be recommended to you are brooms (besoms), wands, knives, swords, spears, chalices, cauldrons, herbs and crystals, divination tools, candles, and smoke. Let's look at each of these and their traditional uses.

I will divide them into some useful categories—ceremonial, getting through your aura, clearing your work area, and adding fuel or clarity.

Ceremonial

Some ceremonial tools are chalices and cauldrons (though cauldrons are darned handy for burning paper spells). Chalices come in many shapes and sizes, and as with all the suggestions and ideas in this book, you should find the one that works best for your work. Chalices are used to hold liquids used during ceremonies—wine, water, and the like. To hold liquids during energy work, I prefer a stout pitcher if it must be poured or a glass canning jar if the liquid only needs a container.

Most people can't imagine a witch without a cauldron, and most magic-workers have at least one. We think of it as a magical tool, but a cauldron is just a pot that was originally used for cooking, for laundry, and for making medicine. You can drive past country homesteads and see a fat cauldron set in the yard, full of flowers. This may have been the laundry pot of a previous generation—too heavy to move, too sentimental to give away, and too old-fashioned to use. My first working cauldron was a cast-iron beanpot with a smear of paint on one side. It came from a thrift store near my office when I worked downtown. Since those early days, I've assembled a few more the same way, in addition to some that were thoughtful gifts from savvy friends.

As with any tool, choose containers for your workings that are practical to use and affordable for your budget. An expensive chalice or cauldron will not make your magic any better or any worse. If your mother has an old cast-iron beanpot that she's throwing out, she may be handing you the exact tool you need.

Getting through Your Aura

The energetic field that surrounds your body is often referred to as your *aura*. It is generally believed that sending the energy of your chosen working requires a tool that pierces your personal energy field. The tools most often used for this include wands, knives, swords, and spears. These can be used like lightning rods to pull energy in and to send your energetic intentions to their desired destination.

Wands are most often made of wood but not necessarily. Wood is believed to be a good conductor of energy and is usually affordable and effective. Wands are also made of several metals—steel, cast iron, aluminum—as well as glass. They are often topped with a particular stone that has conductive power.

Magical knives (including the ubiquitous athame) are of two types: ceremonial and utilitarian. A ritual knife is most often used to cut through the energy field of a cast circle. It is generally worn at the waist in a scabbard, as part of ceremonial ritual wear. The curved blade of a boline is meant for cutting herbs and is shaped like a sickle or reaping hook. It often has a white (bone) handle.

You may see swords and spears at magic-worker and Pagan gatherings, but these tools are less often used in simple magics.

They belong more to the world of ceremony and less to the homely practices of the witchery we are exploring.

I have several of each of these tools but rarely use them anymore.

Try utilizing them if you feel your work isn't reaching the desired target—your shielding may be so strong that the intentional energy can't get past it.

Clearing Your Work Area

Much of your work may be performed in your kitchen or other multiuse space. This may require clearing the energy in that work area. Two useful tools for this are your handy broom or besom and special smoke materials.

In addition to cauldrons, the tool most often associated with witches is the broom, the besom. A broom is an immensely practical tool: there is nothing that does the work of clearing a space like a broom. A broom is made up of two parts—the head (or bristle) and the handle (or stick). Before the advent of modern broommaking, a broom's handle was usually retained when the head was replaced, and the bristles were replaced as often as needed by easily attained materials. When shopping for a broom, it is best to find a handle that fits both your hand size and your height.

Sweeping up—including up the walls in the corners of the room—shakes the existing energy and sweetens it. Drifting smoke from a bound stick of dried herbs or from incense on a charcoal brick continues the process of clearing and sweetening. I may follow that up with a drop of dressing oil on the workspace and the doorways and windows in the room.

Adding Fuel or Clarity

Divination tools and candles are other materials that aid in your spellwork. Candles can be dressed with special oils as a vessel for your harvested energy. And all those divination tools may help you clarify and set your intention for the work.

Take It Slow

Review all these fun things and then decide what you'd like to start working with. I don't recommend you buy all the things at once and leave them in a box until you are ready. Get each tool and spend time getting to know what it does and whether it agrees with you. You may not know that last part for a while, so give it time. I will always suggest that you take your time and go deep. It will help you be a better magic-worker, and that level of focus will serve you well as a regular old human too.

As my practice has matured, I've found that the tools most often used are things that are hanging out in my house or in my garden—soil, gravel, rainwater, mica, red clay. Because the secret that will be revealed again and again in these pages is this—setting a strong intention and aiming your direct action to that intention is most of the magic you'll ever need. That means that our other necessary tools are our hands, hearts, and the strength of our will, our desire.

My Favorite Tool: Magic Hands

I should think of a more lyrical or edgy name for this set of tools, but I've always called it "magic hands." I often use my hands in this way and they are tools that I always have with me. Magic hands is your ability to use your hands as both a divination tool and a discernment tool, and I have used them in this way for so many years that this is one of those techniques that I need to reverse engineer in order to explain it.

Begin by rubbing your hands together to warm them up and to get the energy flowing. Stretch your hands out, fingers up and palms out, and let them guide your steps. An example: You've misplaced your keys. You always put them in the same place, and they are not there. You are flustered and mildly concerned. You need to go out in about five minutes and where the heck are your darned keys? You grow more flustered, which makes it hard to think back to the last time you used your keys—and why aren't they in the bowl on the table? More frustration, rising fear.

Stop. Breathe. Ground. Rub your hands together and visualize your keys. Place your hands in front of you with palms out and feel the room around you. Breathe. Follow your intuition and your hands to the jacket you don't wear all the time, the one hanging behind the door. Yeah. Check the pockets and find your keys.

This may work because on some level you know where you left your keys, but you don't remember where. By grounding, centering, and bringing your attention to the task at hand, you up your chances of success. It's practical, useful magic, the kind that gives you confidence in your ability as well as finding your keys in time to leave the house for work. I think this practical technique is similar to dowsing and to working a pendulum, two things I often say I can't do. Or can I? Using my magic hands to discern the answers and locations is an awful lot like dowsing.

As you progress in this work, you'll find magic hands is good for so many things. And you will go beyond the place where you are calming yourself so your subconscious can inform your need. When you are setting up a working, magic hands will help your discernment process about the appropriate ingredients for success. Your body knows, and one of the key pieces of magical knowledge is to trust what your body is telling you and to trust your intuition, your gut. I know this is hard. We live in a competitive culture that doesn't inspire trust and many of us have personal histories that make trust problematic. It is immensely valuable to learn this cellular-level personal trust. We have all made mistakes in the past and we will continue to make mistakes going forward because we are humans. Far too often, we could have mitigated the results of our personal mistakes if we had only trusted our intuition about a person, an event, an experience. As I tell my tarot clients far too often—I know you are in love, but that dumpster fire is not your twin flame. Listen to your intuition.

NOW YOU TRY

The discussion of tools in this chapter reminds us that we may choose to work with dozens of specific implements or with none at all.

What tools do you use? Have the tools you regularly use changed over the years? Try going into a wooded area and seeing if a particular stick speaks to you. Spend time with it and try to determine if it is a useable tool for your practice. When in an area of river stone or gravel, observe if there are stones that you are drawn to. Do you feel you should take them with you to your home?

> Hint: It is perfectly okay to choose a tool for its beauty. I have a bone-handled boline that I rarely use but love for the sheer beauty of it—and it looks cool hanging from my belt.

Chapter 4
Natural Born

Were you born with it? I grew up with an expectation that I would have some kind of magical gift as I matured. My great-aunts on my mother's side were known for their precognitive dreams, hands-on healing, and other abilities that seemingly just happened. It wasn't called "magic" but was understood to be a sacred gift and they were vessels for a greater power. I wrote about this in my first book, *Staubs and Ditchwater*, and have subsequently talked about it in classes and presentations.

If you believe, as I do, that the world is inherently magical, it makes sense to think that all of us born into this enchanted place must be trailing our own magic in our wake as we wander through life here. If you still harbor the notion that there is something mundane about everyday life, you may doubt that you can do magic in any real way. Let's try to disabuse you of that notion in this chapter—because I think you were born with it and only need to bring out and heighten what you already have.

Any set of skills and abilities is sharpened through practice, an idea I will reinforce throughout this book. Look at music as an example. My grandmother insisted that I had piano lessons from an early age. She was a naturally gifted player with an excellent ear, one of those blessed souls who could hear a piece of music a couple of times and sit down at the piano and play it. It grieved her, however, that she couldn't read music better. She wanted someone in the family who was properly trained to do what she did naturally.

I was destined to disappoint her because playing the piano was not my passion and I did not have her natural gift. I dutifully learned to read music and went through years of lessons, but I never played with the joy my grandmother did, moving easily between Chopin and "The Glow-Worm." Hers was the real miracle—I was a yeoman, doing a job I could do competently but not brilliantly. I suspect if I had had her gift as well as her support, I would have been a concert pianist.

She also had a beautiful singing voice and took voice lessons late in life when she had both the money and time to dedicate to it. I called her Mimi because she would sing scales while holding me, me-me-me-me-me-me-me-me. Her teacher—himself a retired opera singer—marveled at the quality and depth of her tone, as well as her control over her instrument. But she was the baby of a large family who married an alcoholic and fed her family during the Depression by taking in ironing and mending, in her tiny mill village house. She sang in her church choir, not the Met.

This story illustrates my point about magical ability and the skills required to do what we've come to call magic. The thing I actually inherited from my grandmother and her family was the ease with which magic came to my fingertips, meeting my needs with a native ability to achieve my intentions.

I also sing a bit.

When I was growing up, there in my peculiar family was an expectation that I would have some kind of magical gift as I matured. I have since encountered many people here in the southern highlands of Appalachia whose families have similar gifts, though many of these people have been warned from an early age that these gifts are not to be trusted and are, in fact, the dangerous tentacles of a satanic power. As a result, their abilities have been actively discouraged through the threat of hell's eternal damnation and their skills have been left to languish. It is much more difficult to dig deeply enough to retrieve them when this has happened.

This isn't limited to my home region, of course. As I travel to festivals and conferences, I encounter people from every walk of life who tell the odd stories of growing up entwined with these energies around them, like a friendly cat stropping the legs. For most, there was not much training. If one was lucky enough to grow up in an open-minded family not ruled by the specter of hellfire, there was usually curiosity and some amusement, treating it like some charming parlor game. "Little Helen is going to tell you the dream she had last night, and we will see if it comes true!" The laughter inevitably changed when Little Helen's dreams became prophecy. She would be told to keep them to herself until the event occurred, and then she was allowed to say she had a dream about it. Too few were seen as the prophets they were and consulted as such, especially the girl-children. It is gratifying to meet a person who grew up with these gifts, uses or once used them, and has passed them on to children, grandchildren, or students.

Humility

Social media reminds us to check our egos, even though every social media platform is a theater of ego, costumed and shouting. Never mind those forums; we are here to learn some old ways and to adapt them to our modern lives in ways that make sense.

There is an understanding in my Appalachian culture that the power and authority for all these practices is a gift—one that flows through and is shaped by the practitioner. This is often expressed as a humility about the work that is often missing in modern magical cultures. Perhaps it is the difference between "high magic" and "low magic": high magic as a ceremonial style of working and low magic as the work of hedge witches and root folks. But I have noticed in my years of being a public witch that there are plenty of people who will brag about how talented or powerful they are without showing any real signs of either thing.

Social media feeds are filled with inexperienced people who have developed strong brands but not strong techniques. We don't need to do that. We don't need to prove anything by prancing around exclaiming our never-fail witchery. There is a big difference between being confident and being arrogant. Arrogance is never required, and your skill level will speak for itself.

Humility is not very popular these days. Nor is homeliness, another subject I love to explore—the idea that hearth and home are central to our well-being as humans. Here's a little secret, though, which I happily share with you—when you become adept in these practices and are a confident and proper witch, you will walk humbly in the world because you know exactly what you are capable of and where your true strengths lie. You won't be in competition with those around you and will be merely curious about how they do what they do. You will compare notes and swap stories—colleagues, not competitors.

Try some humbleness on for size and see how it suits you. Imagine walking through the world connected with the land beneath your feet and the sky arcing above you. I think you will find it a very good feeling indeed and worth all the practice.

Now let's engage in a discussion about specific techniques with a clear statement about your use (or not) of the skills. Following are some of the latent skills you may have lying under the surface of your everyday life—skills you want to hone, to sharpen, and use. My language about these things comes from the generations before me, and I will translate as necessary. They are old-fashioned and quaint now but held power to those who used them. Note well—these skills can be sharpened if you already have the knack for them, and I encourage you to do that.

However, you are not compelled to engage in any of the following activities, whether you seem to have a gift for it or not. Often such insight and connection are a troublesome burden that is better left to others to claim and use. Read through the chapter, if you find it interesting, but don't feel there is an obligation to do these—or really anything we discuss throughout these pages. Let your curiosity guide you to learn and practice while being aware that not all practices fit best on all people.

Overlooking

This is sometimes called "remote viewing," and there are interesting rumors that the US Central Intelligence Agency had a program to train likely subjects so the agency could monitor what those dang Commies were up to during the Cold War. I suspect modern satellites have made that unnecessary as a spy tool. I know it from old stories of grown children moving away from the home place before phones, Zoom, and FaceTime. In my mind, it is the province of older people keeping in touch with the son in prison, the daughter who married and moved across the country, and the estranged family member who was still cherished. The techniques vary from closing your eyes and reaching out energetically to the longed-for one to the tried-and-true method that I learned as a child.

It is best to try this at night until you've gotten the hang of it. Set up a mirror on a table facing you. Set a low candle between where you are sitting and the mirror, so that the flame is reflected in the mirror. Turn the lights off in the room and make sure the windows are covered.

Light the candle and calm your thoughts through deep breaths and solid grounding. Allow your gaze to soften and look past the reflection of the candle into the reflected darkness of the room behind you. Think of the person you are trying to connect to. Speak their name softly and gently. Wait patiently because it may take some time to make the connection.

The purpose of this remote viewing is to satisfy your mind that all is well with your loved one, and when you sit down at the table with that intention, you will find a greater rate of success. But if you're spying on your ex to see who she's with now or some other trivial reason, it is usually less successful. This has been reported to me by people who work regularly with the technique, but I don't know why the intention has an impact on the success rate.

If you are new to this technique, you may choose to set a time limit on those early learning sessions to avoid the sort of frustration that can lead to dropping it as part of your practice because you feel you don't have a knack for it or that it's too hard. You can set your phone or your kitchen timer for ten minutes and go from there.

You may see shadowy moving images at first, and it sometimes helps to sit at an angle to the mirror. It will feel as if you are looking into a corner. And softening your gaze is a helpful beginning technique. Let me explain that a bit. Back in the 1980s, there was a craze for these interesting graphics called Magic Eye. If you looked directly at the image, it didn't make any sense and was a mass of colors. But if you looked at it from the side you could see the image. Likewise, if you squinted or unfocused your eyes, that action often brought the image into 3D focus. If you wear eyeglasses, you may soften your gaze by taking off your glasses

Since this technique is also helpful in other forms of scrying, let's look at those next.

Divining with Reflective Surfaces

This is another skill that seems to pass down through families and is easily strengthened to be useful. This technique is called scrying and is handy for clearing the mind and focusing it, pulling it into alignment with heart and soul. Most of us are familiar with reading a crystal ball—it's a wildly popular part of entertainment culture. From Auntie Em seen through the Professor's crystal ball clutching her chest in the 1939 film *The Wizard of Oz* to the palantír in J. R. R. Tolkien's *The Lord of the Rings* trilogy, the idea that one can peer into a reflective surface and see the future or events happening at a distance is firmly set in our cultural consciousness.

Any reflective surface will do, once you've gotten familiar with the technique, and you may be someone for whom this happens easily though often unbidden. We pass in front of reflective surfaces all the time, mostly in the form of glass in windows and mirrors. If you are someone who "sees" things that are not an actual reflection, you may want to harness this skill a little more firmly.

Still water is also an effective tool for scrying, though we tend to encounter pools of still water less often in the workaday world. A walk along the beach may reward you with a tidal pool ripe for gazing. You may also choose to create a stand in your yard that holds a bowl of rainwater. Having such a tool permanently set up will give you an excuse to go out on a moonlit night and see the magical sight of the full moon shining from a small pool.

Most of us are more likely to catch our reflection in the car window as we are getting in or out or in the display window of a store that we see from the sidewalk. Most of us can't resist checking our reflection and being cheered by how we look or critical of that new haircut that isn't terribly flattering.

As with the overlooking outlined previously, it is best to set time aside for scrying, instead of letting it be a catch-as-catch-can thing that happens sometimes when you least expect. The point of all this instruction is to give you some useful techniques to apply to your practice of witchcraft, after all. It can be terribly disconcerting to flash on something that requires your attention when all you want to do is put gas in the car.

You might also consider a crystal ball. A few years back I decided to try my hand at reading a crystal ball, following the gift of one from an interior designer friend who'd gotten it to "stage" a house newly placed on the market. The homeowner was sure that this decorative item would spoil the prospects (i.e., lower the potential profit) for the house, so my friend was stuck with it. He called me to ask if I had one and how one went about telling fortunes with it. I gave him a brief lesson on scrying, something in which he had no interest. He interrupted me partway through my spiel and asked if I wanted the damn thing. I said yes, naturally.

I ultimately inherited a very nice crystal ball with a tiny imperfection deep in its interior. It came with its own teakwood stand and I keep it covered on the shelf under my home altar. My main form of divination is cards, but I take the ball out periodically to keep my skills sharp. I find that it works best for me as a remote viewing tool and not as a way to see what's going to happen next.

If you have a crystal ball, you can try the following steps with me. If you don't have one, you can try setting up a glass of water in the same way and try this scrying technique with that.

Take the ball off its stand and place it on a piece of dark fabric. I prefer a non-shiny fabric and have a large square of black linen that works well. Next set a candle to your right and turn off most of the lights in the room. Sit quietly for a moment, grounding yourself and setting the intention of seeing what you need to see. Bend over the ball or glass, looking down into it. Relax your eyes and see what shapes emerge from the glass, then allow the rest of the image to take shape around that.

As with overlooking, try to relax and see what you see. Don't try to understand it, only observe, and note as much detail as possible. After the session is finished, write down all that you saw. Your mind will work on what you saw, and you can return to the images later for a clear interpretation. If you connect with scrying, you might want to keep a little notebook or a file with what you see, how long the sessions last, and your interpretation of what you see. It can be helpful to review your progress and see how far you've come. Scrying works best if you approach it with curiosity and don't put pressure on yourself to perform.

Still-water scrying is done in much the same way, and I have a scrying table set up in the backyard, near a bramble hedge. It's an odd thing—a '60s era beige plastic chair with its metal legs missing that sits in the top of a metal barrel and is filled with rainwater. It is the right height for me to bend over and peer into the surface of the water. The setting is quite magical, perched as it is in the corner of the hedge. The moon is often reflected there and, when full, makes a perfect opportunity for gazing.

Water Witching

This has little to do with witching in the modern sense of the word. *Witching* was used for anything that didn't seem to have its source in the workaday world, as though it implied a connection to supernatural powers. Water witching is the ability to find water underground and is employed to also find underground water lines and other buried things (electric lines, sewer lines, and the like). It has been used to discover lost graves in family cemeteries and track the foundations of ruined buildings in old settlements.

It is a form of dowsing and is sometimes referred to in that way. The dowser may use dowsing rods—wire sticks that are held lightly, one in each hand—and walks in the chosen area, holding the rods in front of her body. The rods will dip when the desired but hidden object is discovered. In the case of finding an underground spring or aquifer in order to sink a well, this technique can save both time and money for the homeowner.

Divining with Cards

I began reading cards around the age of twelve and started out with regular playing cards. I moved on to tarot cards in high school when I got a book of the *Pop/Rock Tarot* major arcana with perforated pages at a Scholastic book fair at school. I still have a few of them all these years later. They live on one of my altars as a reminder of all the things that made me the witch I am today. I hope you will keep trinkets too—talismans to remind you of your journey into all the enchanted things.

My best advice about cards is that you pick a deck whose artwork appeals to you and live with it for a good long time. The present day is filled with so many choices beyond the Smith-Waite one, often called the Rider deck, though I prefer to honor the artist who created the image: Pamela Pixie Colman Smith. All those choices can be confusing. Go to a well-stocked shop, if possible, and take your time looking at the decks. One will probably stand out to you, and when it does, pay for it and get to know it. If it is a tarot deck, it is divided into two parts—the major and minor arcana. Start with the majors, sometimes traditionally called the "greater trumps," and get to know them, card by card.

Sit with each card and look at the artwork, studying both the image and how the image affects you, speaks to you. Then study them two by two and see how the combination speaks to you. Continue in this way until you've worked your way through the major arcana. Then try laying out three cards, face down, and turning them over one by one. What do you see? What do you feel? How do the cards interact with each other?

After you feel confident about the majors, dive into the minor arcana, which are a little easier. The traditional suits are pentacles, wands, cups, and swords. See what each suit means to you and check the book that came with the cards. I do not advise using the book as you are learning, except as a reference when you get stuck. There is simply no way you can memorize the meaning of each card or the meaning of each card in relation to another and to all the others. Working through the meanings of each suit will take you a long way toward doing successful readings, but once you have a sense of the cards, don't be shy about small readings for yourself and your friends. It will build your confidence and make you a better reader.

There are also divination card systems that are not tarot, such as oracle decks, standard playing cards, and Lenormand. I learned to read cards with a ragged playing card deck. They are easy to find and inexpensive. Oracle decks come in a dizzying array of styles and numbers of cards and often have helpful instructions for the card's meanings on the face of the card. Lenormand has a more recent history than tarot and has fewer cards. If you choose a deck that is not a tarot one, proceed in the same way, card by card. As before, pick a deck whose art touches you and spend time with it until it is a tool that fits your work.

Prophetic Dreams

We use the word *precognitive* now, which has fewer religious overtones. These are the dreams that come to us in what I call the country of Night. This is often the first of these gifts to surface in children because it requires no training or deep understanding of meanings. It is perfectly natural for a child to talk about dreams at breakfast and wonder what they mean. It is only a step away from Mom remembering the dream days later when the events of the day seem to be much like the child's report on her dream.

But some families are confused by such a gift or even assume it to be something unsavory, evil, and dangerous. The child may be discouraged from telling her dreams and frightened into silence. I meet with people all the time who have suppressed the dreams of their childhood and now want to know how to get that ability back.

There are several kinds of dreams, and it is well to discern the difference. I refer to them as prophetic, problem-solving, and making sense of the day.

Prophetic Dreams: Prophetic dreams are the ones that seem odd or significant, that use parts of daylight life to inform us about what is coming up. They often appear distorted visually or aurally as if the video is off-kilter. Most people who have these recurring dreams throughout their lives recognize them for what they are as soon as they open in the dreaming world. This encourages the dreamer to pay special attention.

Problem-Solving Dreams: These are the ones that come to us to work out a problem that's bothering us, something we need an answer for. Most people have found that they can go to sleep with a problem that somehow gets solved in the night, as our subconscious keeps looking for solutions as our bodies get the rest they so need.

Making Sense of the Day Dreams: Making sense of the day allows our imaginations to run wild, playing out scenarios from books or films or replaying images from recent days. They bring us new ideas, different viewpoints, and sometimes take us to places where we can relax and refresh our souls.

As you work with your dreams, you will get good at determining which dream is which and how to work with them. There are allies too. Keep a pen and a scrap of paper or a notebook by your bed and jot down any fragments of dreams that come to you the moment you wake. They don't need to be detailed. Simple notes will refresh your memory.

It will also help if you practice good sleep hygiene. No electronics a half an hour before sleep, some gentle stretches, and wearing comfy sleep clothes are all part of good sleep hygiene. A small pillow full of lavender is helpful and a warm cup of herbal tea will give you something in your tummy to see you through the night.

The useful and easy-to-grow herb mugwort is a well-known ally in both sleep and dreams. It's part of the *Artemisia* genus, which also includes *Artemisia absinthium*, the herb that gives us absinthe. *Artemisia vulgaris* is common mugwort and is found naturalized in many places. It is well-known as a dream tonic.

Used as a tea, dabbed on pulse points in oil form, or stuffed fresh inside your pillowcase, mugwort will help adjust your dreams. If you suffer from bad dreams or night terrors, mugwort can help bring them down to a manageable level. If you want to remember your dreams, mugwort can aid you to better do that.

There are many other relaxing herbs that will help you step away from the stresses of daily life and allow you to indulge in the rest that night and sleep offer. Consult a local herbalist for a good list of helpful sleepy-time herbs, and always check with your doctor before beginning any herbal regimen.

Prophetic Visions

These are the daydreams we were chastised about when we gazed out the window in class. Like you, I was one of those children who was frequently caught not "paying attention" when I was actually paying attention to something other than what the adult standing in the front of the room had decided was important.

These images are worth the time it may take to cultivate them. I divide them into two kinds: escaping the current boredom and proto-trance.

Escaping the Current Boredom: This is self-explanatory and is a handy skill but not necessarily "magic." You are in a situation where you are trapped either by a relentless (and mindless) talker or by a meeting (usually work related) that doesn't require your input, only your warm body to make up numbers or fill the space. If it is the former (and you don't have a handy "sorry, I hear my mom calling" excuse), focus on the person's chin and nod occasionally, trying not to lose track of the thread of the monologue. If you are in a Zoom where you can't close the video or in an in-person meeting, rather than peer at the phone in your lap, seat yourself comfortably and focus your eyes to the farthest edge of the table in front of you. Try for a neutral facial expression—a slight smile makes you look guilty, and a slight frown will have the speaker focused on you to bring you into compliance with the agenda. What would you rather be doing? If this is taking time away from projects that inspire you, go over the next steps in your head and jot down notes as they come to you. I'm thinking we could call this "lucid daydreaming." Make sure to come up for air every five minutes or so and, as with the previous example, try not to lose the thread of the conversation so when you hear your name unexpectedly, you can nod for a few seconds as you prepare your noncommittal answer.

Proto-Trance: The second type, a proto-trance, can happen to you unbidden, if you are a person who already has some inclination toward that. Our working definition is a vision that comes to you while you are awake and delivers you to a place set outside of time and space. Such a vision may take only moments to unfold—much like a dream does—but leave you with a profound sense of having been transported to a space where you received needed information.

If these visions come too often or in places that endanger you, you must create boundaries around the experience. There is often a helpful aura that warns you such a vision is forming and soon to appear. This aura may be in the form of an intuition or feeling, a sound, or a change in your vision. Learn to recognize your particular signal through conscious observation. Once you've determined the aura, teach yourself the way to either accept or reject it. Boundaries in all parts of life are important and healthy. If you are in a place—physically and emotionally—to act as a vessel for the vision, breathe yourself to a sense of calm and allow it in. You can imagine yourself opening a gate and sitting down in a front garden. Most visions are not dark and horrifying, despite what you may have read in horror fiction or seen in films.

If you choose to reject the vision, you can choose from several protocols or create your own. You can change your position, change your breathing, eat something, or ground in whatever way works best. Speaking the word *no* aloud, perhaps with a gesture, also works. You can also postpone the vision—not now. But if you keep postponing the vision, you may find that visions come less often and may finally stop coming to you at all. That is certainly a choice that can be made. Visions are a responsibility and can be a liability, if you choose to share them with the people around you who are not as receptive to that particular gift.

Discerning the meaning of visions is a skill unto itself, and it generally comes with the ability to receive visions. I have found that the interpretation, like dream interpretation generally, is highly individual. A symbol may speak differently for you than for another person seeing the same symbol. Because of this, a standardized approach usually doesn't work well. Trust your intuition for the meaning and then double-check it against the message to test for accuracy.

Spirit Communication

The first thing to remember is that there are many kinds of spirit beings, and the first thing to forget is every movie you ever saw about ghosts. As I tend to do, I'll begin with a story, this time about my mother. She always said the "witch stuff" didn't come to her but I suspect that was because she had a problematic relationship with her mother, who reveled in all the family practices (and was my chief source for my own later exploration). She didn't have the healing hands or the weird dreams. But she often talked about her childhood in the same neighborhood I live in now. It is a small mill village made ragged by urban renewal and gentrification. But in the early Depression years, it was a lively enclave of working-class people who drank too much and worked too hard, often dying young (as my biological grandfather did in this same neighborhood). My mother told us how she had given her aunt a fatal heart attack by throwing a rubber snake in her lap. She told the story in a self-deprecating and humorous way, but I always felt she carried some guilt about it, no doubt because the grown-ups in the family made her feel it really was her fault. That's how families react sometimes. I'm sure she was sent out of the house while her aunt was tended to and only brought back in when the body was cooling. She was young and had no siblings.

The fascinating part came later, after the funeral for her mother's sister. She was outside once again doing the sorts of things that mill children did when they weren't in school or working in the mill. I imagine her watching fat clouds in the sky and letting her mind wander as it would. After a time, she realized there was something unusual in the clouds and peered intently into the sky. She swore she saw her late aunt—the one she'd "killed" with a rubber snake—floating on a cloud. The image seemed solid in her young mind, and she fetched an adult, one no doubt still grieving the sudden loss of the beloved aunt.

My mother was whipped that time, for lying. Whichever adult had been summoned, they couldn't see the image floating heavenward. Perhaps my mother felt so guilty about "murdering" her aunt that she daydreamed her vision, but she swore as an adult that she saw her aunt in the clouds and assumed the image had disappeared when others came out to verify it. This was the beginning of my mother's work with discarnate energy beings as well as her lifelong fascination with ghosts and spirits. If she had been born two generations before, she would have been a Spiritualist, of that I have no doubt. Spiritualism was all the rage from the Victorian era into the 1950s. The movement is based on the idea that the dead still exist in the spiritual form and can be engaged in conversation, for the benefit of the people still living. It is still a vibrant movement, though it has fallen from the heights of popularity it once enjoyed.

We visited many rumored ghost sites when I was a child, and she was the one who suggested a séance after a few beers on a Friday night. My mother had stories of her own encounters with spirits, and that normalized the idea of convening with the dead and, in addition to that, contacting the spirits who were not and never had been human.

Spirit work is a particularly tricky bit of witchery and not everyone is suited to it, even if they have the skills to reckon with these folks. As I have noted throughout this section, it is important to remember that you are under no obligation to follow a path, even if it seems to have been laid out for you.

For simplicity's sake, I will divide spirit beings into two sections: those who were once human and have stayed past their apparent death, and those whose essence has always been noncorporeal and nonhuman.

Once Human

I am not well versed in the modern lore of ghost hunting, nor do I watch those television shows in which an effort is made to frighten the living through a series of grainy and vague videos and important-looking machinery. I have been on ghost walks in several old cities and have occasionally spotted a ghost that the tour guide apparently did not see. One such tour in my hometown prompted me to offer my own version of a ghost tour. I did for a couple of years. I told tales from local history, invited people to peer into dark crannies, and ended at the pub for a beer and a discussion.

In my work as the village witch, I get called out on a regular basis to verify a homeowner's opinion that the house is haunted. Mostly they aren't. Mostly the person who contacted me is the issue and has a vivid imagination, a need for attention, and sometimes an undiagnosed mental illness. In those cases, I act as counselor for the one who called me and do a thorough energy clearing of the affected house. That is often all that is needed.

Never Human

In recent years, I have developed a lively side practice with the land spirits in my area. Even when I travel, I seem to have a knack for sensing their presence, which is almost always a delight. I find them to be generally helpful—especially in the garden and on the farm—and early on realized their lust for brightly colored and artificially flavored candies.

This work is not, strictly speaking, magical, but it often is considered an important part of a magic-worker's skillset. Doing this work effectively will require you to be focused, open minded, and able to discern subtleties in the area around you. It is helpful if you are sensitive to temperature because a sudden or unexplained coldness is sometimes a sign to watch for.

Animal Whispering

You may remember a romantic novel from several years back called *The Horse Whisperer*. It helped normalize the idea that humans can communicate successfully with other species of animals. When I was growing up in rural North Carolina, most animal whisperers were women or girls, and that was certainly true of me. I didn't have any training, but I was around animals all the time—cats, dogs, domestic and wild birds, horses, cows—you get the picture. I was also a solitary child and found (still find) the company of animals some of the very best company.

Most communities now have someone who is an "animal communicator" of some sort, but it wasn't such a big deal back in the day. Our animal companions mostly ran free at our sides, and we shared so much of our time with them in a natural state. Dogs and cats had access to the inside of the house and to the yard outside, often with little supervision. These animals were working animals—cats kept rodents at bay and dogs did their best to repel larger trespassers, especially the human ones.

Our animal companions now are housebound for good reason. Most of us live in neighborhoods where the houses are close together and neighbors also live interior and housebound lives. Animals no longer have jobs, except as service or companion animals. They get bored easily, they have emotional issues, sleep issues, eating issues because—again, like most human animals—they don't get enough of the right sort of exercise and companionship.

These companion animals become family members, and giving your dog the minimum of training benefits both of you. Bathroom training, knowing when and where food and water will be set, not allowing destruction of property, good manners (no biting or jumping)—all these will make living with a nonhuman animal a pleasure and not a burden.

If you have this gift, you may know what the animals around you are thinking, and you may be able to share with them what you are thinking too. These animals are the best place to start establishing direct communication. When you are sitting quietly together, reach out with your mind and see if you can connect with your animal companion.

Words to the wise—if you take your canine companion into your neighborhood or for a walk in the park, please keep them leashed and under your voice control. Because so many animal companions have been badly trained or indulged, many people are afraid of a loose dog—and rightly so.

Plant Whispering

Our gift for anthropomorphizing any spirit being is also a sign of our species' chauvinism, or maybe our thwarted imaginations. Those people who seem to communicate with the plants around them are generally less inclined toward the winged beings separate from the plants themselves. If you want to check your skills, it is best to start with large old plants—our eldest green relatives, the trees.

The same open-mind protocol that you used with animals can also work with plants, especially trees, if you choose to start there. Find an older tree that lives in a place you can access, a place that affords a little privacy. Spend time with the tree in all sorts of weather and throughout the seasons. Deciduous trees are especially nice because they look different in each season. As an animist, I often speak about the acknowledged kinship that connects everything to the web of all life, and that is always a good place to start as you work with other beings in the world. We humans have been too long at the business of exploiting and taking, and it is time to understand on the most profound levels what it means to be one with the world with which we live.

Come with me onto the muddy path that leads into the woods, to the Madron Well. It is an ancient site in Cornwall, a short bus ride from Penzance and home to a famous cloutie display. On the right-hand side of the path is a windbreak of tall trees. The walk goes slowly as we place our feet carefully and anticipate this storied place. (I had heard of it years back from one of my teachers, Jyoti Bryan.) It takes some quiet moments to hear the squeaking and speaking trees as they rustle together in the mild wind. With our mind's ear, we discern their voices, a chorus of sounds that suggest caution, advise care, and announce our arrival.

There are people—and you may be one of them—whose mind's ear is attuned to the hum of the plants with whom we share our landbase. The Theosophists (and others, primarily New Age adherents) refer to plant spirits as *devas*, and many people visualize them as tiny, winged figures, similar to Cicely Mary Barker's flower fairies.

You begin by touching the tree, resting your fingers on the bark, feeling the texture. Breathe and ground. See if you can feel what the tree is feeling. This is best done while sitting quietly at the base of the tree and relaxing your focus, feeling the bark on your back. Be patient. Be open. At first you may only get what you feel about the tree and the day and where you are in your life right now. Don't rush it and you will be rewarded with something like extra thoughts in your head. And as you deepen your listening skills, you may hear the soft voices on the air around you.

Halos and Auras

Aura photography is a big deal in some circles. I started seeing auras at about eight and see them to this day. I would ask my mom or elder cousins why there were colors around a particular person's body or body part. Sometimes I would see what seemed to be heat ripples (like you see on a sidewalk on a very hot day), but more often it is particular colors blending into each other. When I asked my mother about it, she didn't understand, and finally my grandmother took me to an optometrist. That turned out to be fortunate because I could only see clearly close up and was given a pair of glasses to see the greenboard at school—a wonderful improvement. I still saw the odd colors but stopped asking other people about them, instead reading all I could and ultimately talking to other people who could see what I saw.

The field sometimes extends far away from the physical body, but sometimes it is held tightly in, close to the body. After years of asking questions and remembering what I see, I understand that if the auric field is tight, the person is ill, depressed, stressed, or all three. The aura is closed in to protect the physical body as best it can.

Sometimes I see a person with a wide and expansive aura. The colors are gently blended at the edges and the veiling of the color is bright and covers the whole body. These people are inevitably joyful, healthy, invigorated, and upbeat. Naturally, most of us fall somewhere in between the two extremes.

Training yourself to see auras can be worthwhile for a couple of reasons. It can help you in dealing with strangers or with acquaintances and friends who seem to be acting out of character. If you are aware of their tightened aura, you can give them the benefit of the doubt and assume they aren't well. (You don't need to see auras to do this, however. Giving people the benefit of the doubt can go a long way to avoid unnecessary drama and the dead-certain feeling that whatever is bothering them is about you. For what it's worth, it almost always is not about you.)

If you are also a healer by nature, you will find ways to analyze the color and pattern and then gently inquire about the person's health. Don't start pointing and shrieking about colors and body parts. No one will appreciate the attention-seeking qualities of that sort of engagement. If the person in question is someone you know well, be gentle and curious.

It is also wise not to broadcast that you see these colors and patterns because everyone who finds out will come stand in front of you demanding that you tell them what their aura looks like. Keep it to yourself as much as possible. Four helpful lessons are to know, to dare, to will, and to keep silent.

Practice by asking a friend to stand with her back to a sunny window. Request that she wear a solid color shirt—I find white is best to start out with. Stand to one side of her and squint your eyes, looking at the area around her shoulder. You may need to reposition yourself several times to see the subtle edge of color hovering over her shoulder.

These auras almost never look like the ones in the photographs, so if you are comparing what you are seeing with Kirlian photography, don't be discouraged. See what you see and learn to detect what the colors and field depths mean. Certainly you can discuss your observations with other people who see them, but don't assume that what they see will equate with what you see. From experience, I can tell you that we often see these images in different ways, with different colors, but the results are the same.

Second Sight/the Sight

It is the stuff of myth and occasional nightmare: the person who has the uncanny ability to know something they have no way of knowing, of seeing what they are not physically close enough to see. Commonly called second sight to distinguish it from the work of our eyes in physical space, several cultures (including my own) refer to it simply as the Sight. Like most skills that are not easily explainable, the Sight is challenged, and its veracity doubted, which is as it should be.

Unlike overlooking, which is a technique that can be tried and developed, the Sight seems to be a skill that we are born with and one that comes unbidden, as the distant event occurs. It is not very helpful, to be honest, and is often more a burden than a gift. In the years before mass communication, it was a good thing to have someone in the family who could sense things at a distance and report on what was seen. But now it is a simple thing to text or call to inform far family and friends of events as they occur. To have the Sight is to have your day interrupted by streams of information that is distracting and emotionally draining. If you have this gift and cannot yet shield yourself from it, it can feel like your workaday life is not your own. It makes it hard to concentrate and to focus on needed tasks, and it can leave the practitioner feeling like a sponge, always absorbing events but never having agency in them. It can be frustrating as well as unnerving.

These knowings often come like a bolt out of the blue and the receiver seems to experience the event for themselves. It is fully formed and complete. You may feel it as a jolt to the head or the stomach with the subsequent information flowing into your consciousness. For many people, it is like a sudden migraine in its intensity and speed but without the pain. Like migraines and seizures, the Sight is sometimes preceded by an aura—a visual event with odd bands of colors or misshapen images. When this happens, the canny recipient may have time to sit down and compose herself before the event uncoils.

If you think you have this ability but aren't sure, spend part of a free and quiet day exploring the feelings in your gut. Visualize that gut feeling rising up to meet your thoughtful self as your awareness flows down into your torso, thought meeting feeling at about your heart level. What am I feeling? Fear? Joy? Pain? Anger? Then let your intellect chew on the feeling by asking yourself the second question: Where is it? This is often an easier question to ask than you might think—our inner directional markers are the things that give us a sense of direction and can aid us in figuring out the direction from which we are receiving. When you are first practicing, you may want to stand in a quiet place and turn slowly, allowing the gut feeling to align strongly with the direction.

The answer to the next question is often harder to discern: Who is it that is being affected by the event? There is usually someone you know and love enmeshed in it, which is why the call gets sent to you to parse. You may see the event clearly or have an understanding of what is happening: a car wreck, a birth, a death, a violent encounter.

When you have determined the what and who, the event is often revealed in its entirety. Sometimes it comes as a visual, as though you are watching the event in real time. Sometimes it is a thought pattern that springs into your mind. Often it stays somewhere in the middle of your body as a kind of general concern—those are the times we say, "I have a bad feeling. Something feels off."

Hands-On Healing

Hands-on healing skill is a kind of intuitive Reiki, I think, and is too often used by charlatans and revival preachers to show off their supposed powers and connections. It covers a wide range of abilities that includes soothing headaches and fevers, removing skin conditions (burns, cancers, warts, etc.), and settling gastric issues, all with the calm application of warm hands to the affected area. Much of it is psychosomatic—a person feels ill but much of the illness is loneliness, and a generous application of good attention will go far in remedying that.

But others are not so easily explained. The old woman who can remove warts by rubbing the area with her thumb, the burn spell that dates back centuries and cools the skin, rubbing the area between thumb and palm to relieve headaches. If you have this ability, you are probably a very busy person. We humans love an easy fix for anything that ails us, whether it is a pill, a colorful bandage, or a gentle and compassionate healer.

ﻌﻌﻌﻌﻌﻌﻌﻌ

NOW YOU TRY

Let me remind you that you are not less of a magic-worker if you didn't grow up seeing auras or having dreams that came true. You can develop any of these helpful skills through consistent and focused practice. If you were born with one or more of these abilities, you may choose to enhance them in the same way—consistent practice. But you may choose to ignore them and let them subside, unused. The skill may be an annoyance, a distraction, and compromise your enjoyment of life, especially when it arises unbidden and uncontrolled. It may be that you will live with a skill for a while and decide it isn't for you. As with all things in this book, the choice is yours.

But where should you begin? I've shared many helpful possibilities. First think about the abilities you may already have and that you may practice. Do you want to make them stronger, more reliable? How would you practice them to be more effective? Then consider what skills you may suspect you have but aren't quite sure. Are there skills here that other family members have or are purported to have, and would they be helpful to learn and improve?

Finally, is there something here that intrigues you and you'd like to try it, as I did with a crystal ball? Give it a go and don't be concerned about your skill level on the first try. If you approach all these techniques with curiosity and a sense of adventure, you may be surprised at what fun it all is. Joy and satisfaction with your work—whichever work you are doing—is important.

Hint: Don't get overwhelmed by the possibilities.

Chapter 5
Preparation Techniques

In this chapter, I will demonstrate the importance of preparation and grounding. I will also share the possible places in our practice for relaxation, stretches, and other ways of getting embodied and for weaving our spirit into our earthy selves for strength and effectiveness. You are adding building blocks to your practice through attention to breathing and relieving stress throughout the body.

When I read the word *preparation*, it sends my mind back in time to ballet classes when I was a child. The general consensus of my mother and grandmother was that I was undeniably clumsy and something must be done about it. I think it was partly undiagnosed poor eyesight and that I was still figuring out gravity—since I spent most of my time outside digging in soil, playing in the creek, and climbing trees. I do recall tripping over the base of one of those portable blackboards in school, but I don't think I fell down. I floundered a bit and waved my arms around but caught myself before I fell on the floor. Nothing to be done except enroll me in ballet, right? I stayed for a few years and came to love it. I still delight in the feel of my body moving through space, and I have the sweet memory of dancing toward a bank of large windows as the sun was streaming in. Today most festivals find me dancing around the bonfire, waving my arms in wild abandon, unaware of any watchers.

Each ballet class began with the instructor saying, briskly, "Preparation!" This meant we were to focus ourselves on the task, train our eyes on the teacher and put our backs, feet, and arms in the appropriate position. We would often go through the five basic positions to make sure those little dancers remembered the basics—First. Second. Third. Fourth. Fifth. Then she repeated "preparation!" and we did the choreography we were learning. It was surprisingly rigorous and there was much repetition. I also think the instructor (or the head of the school) already knew whether any of us were any good or had potential. But it was good discipline and that seemed to be important in those long ago days.

Repetition is key in transferring information from your head to your body, to take an exercise from an intellectual one to a physical one. In the case of magic, it can make the difference between sometimes being effective and being mostly effective. This chapter on the various techniques will give you the tools necessary to go from one to the other. The techniques themselves are simple but it is the practice—the repetition—that will make them stick with you when your world is chaotic and needs to be put in some sort of order that makes sense.

In this and the following chapter, we are going to cover breathing and other relaxation techniques, grounding, energy acquisition and storage, and intentional/focused release of energy. Then we'll turn our attention to shielding and other forms of defensive and offensive magic. These are the calisthenics of magic.

All the following techniques are ones that I use. They are not the only protocols for any of these techniques. You will try them and they will work for you, or you will try them and have to adjust to meet your needs. Such is the nature of the work. This is not engraved in stone, and you are always—always!—encouraged to make these practices work for you, in whatever way is effective. The point is not that you memorize my way to do them but that you have techniques that work for you. I don't need you to ground "my way." I need you to find an efficient way to ground.

Get your sweatpants on. We've got some work to do.

Breathing

We will go through a few styles of breathwork and find one that oxygenates the blood while also relaxing us for our work as magic-wielders and as an aid to meditation. We'll begin with the simplest—deep breathing.

Relaxing the Breath

Lay your hands on your belly and take a slow breath in. If your belly did not move when you inhaled, your lungs probably didn't fill up completely. Rub your belly gently and release the muscles that tighten when you think of the phrase *suck in your gut*. You can also do some gentle patting—laughing helps too. Try that breath again. Inhale and feel your belly gently rise as your lungs fill. You may need to lie down to fully feel the difference, but your goal is to fill your lungs with as much air as they can take in.

Some of us are breathing-challenged, usually through illness. As with any exercise in this section, do the best you can, given the way your body works. This is not about fixing something you cannot correct. It is about your getting as fully oxygenated as possible. To learn more about it, I did an informal interview with my friend Angie C. She is a woman whose chronic obstructive pulmonary disease

(COPD) is best treated with a breathing apparatus that she wears constantly. Since her ability to breathe is already compromised by illness, I wanted to know about her practice. Angie said, "While I am grateful to have to oxygen ... there are days—like when it is very hot or damp—that breathing is hard, even with the oxygen. ... If I use my rescue inhaler and try not to panic, my lungs will open for a few minutes, and I can [breathe deeply]. I do the four-square breathing, but I do three counts each. It's just a matter of making myself relax. I'm still learning."

We are often guilty of concentrating on the breathing-in part and ignoring the breathing-out part, but they are equally import-ant. Once you have the feeling of filled lungs, spend a moment emptying them in the same slow way. Keeping your hands on your belly, exhale as slowly as possible. Take a small pause, then inhale again. If at all possible, breathe through your nose with your mouth closed.

Four-Square Breathing

One way to train yourself in this healthy breathing is an exercise called four-square breathing or box breathing, the technique Angie mentioned and one I use frequently. I do this at the dentist's office, and it is helpful in focusing my attention away from the discom-fort of all the hands that are in my mouth. It is so easy to do, and you can practice it almost anywhere and anytime. The sequence is to inhale, hold the breath, exhale, then rest. We do all of this on a count of four, but most people find themselves stretching it out as a challenge, like when we were kids and challenged each other to see who could hold their breath the longest. When I am working on these warm-up and relaxation sequences, I work my way up to thirteen, which is easy to remember. But as we are mastering this technique, we start with four.

Inhale for a count of four, then hold that breath for a count of four, exhale for a count of four, and relax for a count of four. Then we repeat the sequence: inhale 2-3-4, hold 2-3-4, exhale 2-3-4, rest 2-3-4.

Open-Mouth Breathing

There is a gasping, open-mouthed technique that will energize you and focus your attention on your breathing. I will often combine these two techniques for a full breathwork session. I learned this as a Goddess meditative practice called "Durga breathing," in which you gasp the first syllable of the Divine Name and expel the breath with the second syllable. *Dur-gah. Dur-gah.* Essentially we are filling our lungs quickly and emptying them quickly. Warning—do not do this for more than a few repetitions or you are likely to hyperventilate. Seriously. Four counts of this should be enough to remind you to breathe slowly and evenly. This comes in handy at the doctor's office when you are told to "breathe" so the doctor can listen to your lungs. I did it for my doctor when he complimented me on good breathing, explaining the technique and demonstrating with the two syllables of Durga's name (which led to an interesting discussion of the nature of the Divine).

Try this breathing after a few repetitions of the four-square breathing and return to four-square after. It is a wonderful toner for your lungs, very invigorating.

As you practice your breathwork for magic, always remember that if you feel dizzy in any of the exercises, sit down, slow your breathing, and spend some moments breathing deeply and naturally. In many cases, we are retraining ourselves to breathe in ways that relax our bodies and oxygenate our blood, two important parts of your body doing magic work.

We all breathe in some fashion or another because it is one of the important functions of most living creatures. Breathing is easy for most of us, so easy we may take it for granted. That easy breath may be an unacknowledged luxury when illness strikes, and we are made painfully aware of its importance. We have endured a global pandemic of a SARS-CoV-2 virus that too often ends with the patient being intubated in order to breathe. And how many of us carry EpiPens to ensure that the sting of an insect doesn't spell death through anaphylaxis?

Stretching

With several good breathing techniques in our workbasket, we move on to an old actor's trick for relaxation. For years I began by teaching grounding right off the bat but found that this isn't the natural first step. As with most things, the first step is to get yourself in the right headspace and physical place to learn a new technique. By going through these relaxation and focusing steps, you'll get yourself focused and ready to work.

The world that most of us live in is full of distractions, anxiety, noise, and chaos. We are going to ease into a successful way to ground, a practice discussed in the next chapter, by first removing ourselves psychically from all those annoying things and people that are stealing our focus. Stretching helps accomplish this. Carving out this space for learning is beneficial but sometimes it isn't easy. Give yourself the gift of this self-focused time and it will pay off for you down the road. As we move through the rest of this chapter, we'll look at some physical activities that will benefit your practice and your workaday life.

Checking In on Your Physical Reality

Before beginning, it is important to look at your personal physical realities. Not all bodies move in the same way, some bodies move with pain and some bodies don't move much at all. No judgment, only the physical reality that we've come to live with. Keep these thoughts in mind as we go through these exercises:

1. Adjust these and any other exercises to fit what your body can do.
2. Don't hurt yourself doing something you know you can't or shouldn't. We'll focus on gentle warm-ups and most bodies can do that.
3. These stretches should always be done slowly and gently to get maximum benefit. Think about the way a cat wakes from her nap in the sunny window: she half-rises, yawns into a luxurious stretch, and then sits blinking for a moment before jumping down in search of food or entertainment.

We will stretch our bodies awake and then go in search of energy and magic. And perhaps we will finish with a catnip treat.

Throughout the following exercises, you will be invited to inhale and exhale deeply and slowly with one word: *breathe*. This doesn't mean this is the only place you breathe—you should be breathing throughout. It is a reminder, one that many of us need. We'll cover good and healthful breathing right after the warm-ups. Until then, please breathe deeply and slowly.

In writing this out, sequence by sequence, it looks like quite a workout and a big time commitment, but the reality is that it can take as little as five minutes and feels marvelous. It is worth every moment for the reward you get at the end. You can make yourself a little cheat sheet, if that helps, and break it down segment by segment, but you'll soon find that each stretch naturally leads to the next. We finish with a full-body stretch to which I suggest you add a yawn, a purr, and a treat, in that order.

You will find that this series of stretches can be done separately from each other, depending on where you are. When you're sitting at a traffic light in the car, it feels good to do those shoulder rolls while waiting your turn to go. Standing by your desk or waiting on a colleague may be a good time to go up on tiptoe and settle back, stretching your calves.

Getting Started

To get started with some easy stretching, first clear thirty minutes in the early evening (or the time that works best for your schedule). You have closed yourself off in one room or you have gone to the park or you are in your car, sitting in the parking lot at the grocery store. You are here with the goal of relaxing your body and practicing your breathing. Good for you.

Begin by stretching your hands. Wiggle your fingers and rub your hands together to warm them. Stretch your hands and make your fingers as far apart as they will go. Let them stretch toward the back of your hand—you may see them shaking a bit. Now let them and the rest of your hand go limp. Stretch, relax. Stretch, relax. It feels good, but don't do more than your hands and fingers can stand, especially if you have any sort of muscle pain. The more you do this, the easier it is to move your hands, to use your hands.

Your fingers will probably feel warm and maybe a little tingly. Rub your hands together, connecting the energy of one hand to the other. With your elbows tucking into the sides your body, hold your relaxed hands in front of your body and rotate your wrists. Rotate both hands inward, toward your chest; do this three times. Pause. Now rotate them away from your center three times. Pause. Repeat.

Shoulders and Neck

Many of us keep our tension and anxiety firmly packed into our shoulders and neck, and because of that, it is always a good thing to incorporate shoulder rolls and head turns any time you can during the day. They are simple and can be done anywhere. Start by raising your shoulders up as high as they will go, toward your ears. Hold there for a moment and then let them fall back to the original position. Do this several times. Then gently roll your shoulders forward four times. Pause. Now roll them back, also four times. Pause. Repeat. This feels so good that I tend to do it many times. My massage therapist would thank me if I did that every couple of hours every day.

If it is a particularly stiff-shouldered time—the beginning of gardening season or when I'm building something that requires steady hammer action or heavy lifting—I'll start this whole sequence again from the raise-and-lower-shoulders part.

At this point, slowly and gently turn your head to look right. Then back to the front. Then left the same way. Do this a couple of times, as slowly as you can manage. Then do a few shoulder rolls.

Breathe.

Feet and Legs

If you are in a place where this is practical, draw your attention to your feet. If they are flat on the ground, feel the surface underneath them. Wiggle your toes. Press the ball of your foot into the floor and relax your foot. Press the heel of your foot into the floor and then relax it. For most of us, the direct physical contact with the earth is through our feet, usually when we are shod and often when the earth itself has a covering of concrete, small stones, grass, or asphalt. Teaching your feet to discern the living planet beneath these coverings while you wear shoes is an important piece of your practice and worth taking the time to work through. Bare feet on bare soil is optimal but not always possible or advisable.

Feet come in all sorts of shapes and sizes and in many different levels of sensitivity. Our feet, if we have that sort of mobility, have the enormous responsibility of moving us from place to place safely and efficiently. But we often ignore them until they hurt or otherwise cause us to pay attention to them. I'm a Pisces and it is a truism that as a group we have sensitive feet. In spite of having spent years of my childhood walking barefooted on dirt roads, I now have "Princess and the Pea" feet from years of city life and sensible foot protection. Yes, I do still walk unshod in my garden where I can trust the paths and the soil. And in the house, where the tiniest pebble feels gargantuan. I admire those folks who never wear shoes or wear those lightweight exercise shoes with toe enclosures everywhere, but that is not for me.

Whatever your level of comfort or discomfort, paying attention to the ends of your legs is a smart idea, including applying moisturizer to them at the beginning and end of the day in sandal weather and in winter, and if you turn a dab of foot cream into a massage session, so much the better.

Pressing the ball of your foot down as firmly as you can (which usually means lifting the heel of your foot slightly off the ground), then releasing it and repeating those steps with the heel of your foot (where you slightly raise the toes) will give you a little stretch. This will help with that earth connection and will also help release tension. It is healthful if you have neuropathy in your feet, though you may not get how good it feels. It will help with circulation and that is always a good thing.

Up we go, in a journey up your body that we will certainly use many times in pulling energy from the planet's core. Next are ankles. Let your attention turn to your ankles and we will stretch those a bit. If you are sitting, raise one foot at a time and rotate your ankle, first clockwise then widdershins. Replace that foot on the floor and repeat with the other foot. Now repeat. If you can raise both feet at the same time and do these ankle revolutions, go there now. Right foot and ankle. Left foot and ankle. Both simultaneously. And, of course, repeat. You can also do this standing, but only one foot at a time, please. Levitational warm-ups are not recommended!

Hips

This next part is best done standing, but if standing is challenging for you for any length of time, grab a sturdy chair and hold on to its back for support. You also may find that after doing these warm-ups for a while, you can do them without benefit of chair support. But that isn't important. Standing close to and facing the back of the chair, grip it with both hands. Push your hips to the right and up, bending slightly at the waist. Return to original position, then do the same with your hips to the left. Repeat several times. Now gently push your hips forward, bending slightly at the knee. Return to your original position, then push them back. Repeat. Breathe. Try rotating your hips clockwise, then widdershins. This is done most easily by slightly bending your knees.

Repeat the segment. Hips right. Hips left. Hips forward, then back. Swivel clockwise, then widdershins. Breathe. Repeat.

You may, of course, do this without benefit of chair support. These are belly dance warm-ups and generally make those of us with a little more hip or more belly feel very good.

If you can, bend gently at the waist, letting the arm on the same side dangle toward the floor. Bend right. Return to original position. Bend left. Return. Bend forward. Return. Then look up and bend slightly back. Repeat the sequence, as always, slowly and gently.

Full-Body Stretch

This last sequence is called "picking ripe fruit" and is a full-body stretch. From a standing position with feet apart (try to line them up with your shoulders), stretch your arms out and up. Come up on your tiptoes and stretch your arms as high as you can, then return to original position. Repeat, allowing your fingers to stretch as you reach.

If you are unsteady, you can do this one arm at a time, while supporting yourself with the chair back. If you are in a wheelchair or otherwise sitting, stretch your arms up and out as far as you can reasonably reach. If your legs are mobile, you can stretch them separately from your arms, but if you can do arms and legs at the same time, it feels glorious.

Pelvic Floor Strength: The Magnificent Kegel

I often tie acts of magic to a physical gesture or movement. It helps us remember, and we train our bodies to do the energetic work when the physical signal is given. A helpful and healthful gesture is to tie the work to a signal from the pelvic floor by doing three swift Kegel clenches. Most women know exactly what I mean when I say that word (which is variously pronounced *kay-gull* or *kee-gull*) because this exercise helps keep our innards inside. Hearing or reading the word, most women will reflexively do a few. It's good for you.

These muscles are the ones on the bottom of your torso that you use to stop a stream of urine. They squeeze and release during orgasm. Practice the squeeze and release any time you think of it, both to strengthen those muscles and to draw your attention to the beautifully connected physicality that is you.

Cultivating a Relationship with Your Body

Stretching and breathing are excellent ways to release tension in your body. Hugging a firm pillow—or a firm friend—is another way to "let it go." I stretch up on my tiptoes and then slowly roll down to touch the floor, imagining stress and anxiety flowing out from my fingertips to become energy compost in the soil of the earth. As you consider all the ways you can release these stiffening things, your body and your spirit become more pliable, easy as you walk, and able to receive wisdom from the voices of the natural world.

This was a loving tour through one of your most powerful magical tools: your healthy relationship to your physical body. We have looked at some workarounds for physical limitations as a way to encourage everyone to know and love their bodies. What does this have to do with magical practice? If you are unaware of the way your particular body operates or if you are ignoring your physical self to focus exclusively on your spirit, you are setting yourself up for weaknesses and vulnerabilities in your work. When we work beyond what our bodies can do, we begin to limit the scope of our energetic work. Taking time as we build our craft to recognize the reach and power of the strongest possible support that is our physical selves will be a rich investment going forward.

⁌◦⁍

NOW YOU TRY

Our bodies are another important tool for effective magic, and having a working knowledge of our personal biology is very helpful. We've discussed breathing, stretching, and other ways to really live in these bodies we call home.

In your journal, make some notes about what deep breathing does for your sense of grounding. Does a sense of relaxation and true embodiment make your magical practice more effective, easier?

Hint: Try those Kegel exercises whenever you feel stressed and see how they help in full-body relaxation.

Chapter 6

Grounding

Grounding is one of those words that we often use without benefit of definition, as if we all know what we're talking about. Sometimes a group of people do have a common understanding of the word that jibes, and the group can continue without being picky about an exact definition. We're going to spend a few minutes with the word and some of its meanings and then choose the meaning that best fits what we are doing in our various magical practices.

A few years back, I began to hear the term *earthing* as a synonym for grounding. As long as we agree that these are the same thing, we can use them interchangeably. But they don't seem the same to me. *Earthing* seems to me to be a word we would use to describe putting something into the earth—in other words, burying it. That feels safe in its own way but it doesn't bear the subtle distinction of connecting us to the core of the planet in order to make us stronger and more connected with our source. Earthing is the action that stores something away for future use, like a pirate's buried treasure. Grounding, as I am using it throughout this book, as well as in my classes and workshops, is the act of deeply connecting with the planet's living energy field in order to achieve a stronger stability as well as a more integrated approach to accessing and using the earth's natural energy. This connection helps us wrap our physical and spirit selves together

This chapter gives you myriad ways to achieve that state, and some of them may surprise you, as they did me when I was practicing them. The act and practice of grounding is vital to the way I practice magic and, in fact, live my life. It is so important that finding the easiest and best way to do it is worth all the exploration and experimentation it may take to get that important piece of your personal practice.

But why? Why is it important to perfect a technique for grounding?

Being energetically rooted—like a magnificent oak tree—goes a long way toward easing anxiety and opening yourself to the experience of being embodied, of being in touch with your body. It is the conscious integration of physical self with spiritual self in order to accomplish desired results. This is all in aid of embodying your magical practice and getting you out of your head. Too often our communities are heady folks. They read voraciously and have heads full of the sorts of useless tidbits of information that will help their team win trivia night every time. We know so much interesting stuff and we love to have long discussions on any subject, especially around a firepit. We are also great at feeling all the emotions that course through us: getting angry or outraged over even trivial annoyances, as well as falling in love at the most inconvenient time with the most inconvenient person.

But we are not always aware of what our physical bodies are doing until there is a system failure and we have to pay attention. Much of this is tied to personal histories of shame and abuse as well as a cultural history that often stresses how unimportant the body is because it is only a meat suit for the soul. Conversely, mass media reminds us constantly that our bodies can never be perfect enough to withstand the noxious scrutiny of the arbiters of taste.

Both theses are dead wrong, though church and media will spend fortunes convincing you otherwise. Your body is an incredible instrument, and if I hammer away at one idea in my teaching as a witch and an animist, it is that being embodied is a richly delicious experience and I don't want anyone to miss out on that. Free your body and your soul responds, because they are two of the interwoven parts that make you who you are.

In the sex magic workshop "Honey on the Stones," I invite the participants to touch their bodies, and I model this by touching myself in front of them, beginning usually by wrapping my arms around my upper torso and giving myself a hug. When I first offered this workshop, I was surprised to find that some people are reluctant to touch themselves in public. There are always a few people, fully clothed and daring only to put their hands on their knees, who blush or otherwise exhibit discomfort in doing this simple thing. Modeling my self-hug helps the participants to move to more intimate touch with less guilt and shame. Far too many of us were warned off when we were children, being made to understand that touching oneself was dirty, sinful, or generally wrong. Our culture has much to answer to about the ways we view our bodies, as well as intimacy.

Going to Ground

To beginners and to people who tell me they are not good at grounding, I offer this guided meditation. It generally works but is too long and elaborate for everyday use. I offer a shortcut once this meditation has been mastered.

Everything begins with breathing, with pulling your focus into a narrow space to avoid distractions. You don't need to go through all the breathing steps outlined in chapter 5 again, once you've mastered them. Take a few deep breaths, perhaps closing your eyes.

Wiggle your toes and flex your feet, drawing your attention there. Press your feet into the floor, with the toes, balls of the feet, and heels all pressing downward. Relax your legs and hips, and don't tighten anything in your body. Merely press your feet firmly into the floor.

Now roll your feet around a bit, moving them as best you can, forward and back, side to side, gently, and slowly. We are drawing strong attention to the connection between you and the planet by taking the time to feel the touch of the floor on the different parts of your feet. With feet again pressed down, imagine tiny pale roots growing from the bottoms of your feet and wiggling their way through the rug and the floor and the subflooring, if you are in a building. If you are outside, imagine the layers under your feet— low-growing plants, soil, root system, bedrock. As those tiny roots touch the earth, they move faster, gaining momentum, and they grow stronger. You are setting your energetic roots into the earth, and from there you can feel the answering energy of the planet begin to flow up into your feet, nourishing you with energy in the same way that plants are nourished with water and minerals.

This meditation is a luxury of time that most of us can't afford every day. Because it is so helpful in so many ways, it's a good idea to create shortcuts that get you to a grounded place fairly quickly. A good way to create a shortcut is to feel which part of your foot seems to most easily get to that connection. You will probably find that it's either the ball of your foot or your heel. You can train yourself to use that part by going through the visualization using only that as your contact point until it's something you don't have to think about. It lies in muscle memory.

You can also train yourself to ground by making your hands into soft fists and pressing your nails into your palms or by pressing your palms together as you press your feet downward, but I find this tenses up my body when I need to be open and energetically flexible.

Alternative Methods

If you are someone who uses a wheelchair for mobility or has leg prosthetics, like some of my friends, these exercises (and the ones in the previous chapter) are easily adapted to what you can do and what you can feel. I was curious to learn some possible workarounds, so I talked to Monica A., who has a prosthetic leg. I wanted to know how she grounded—did she use her biological leg and infer the work of the other leg?

Monica said, "I do ground as a part of my practice. It isn't difficult. My leg has titanium in it. Titanium actually conducts nerve signals. My prosthetic leg is a part of me. From when I put it on and even when it's not on. Wheelchair users say the same thing about their wheelchair. Since it is a part of me, I can draw energy and send energy."

She added, "Besides, the energy that is within us and that we draw from the earth isn't bound to our physical bodies as such. It's in my spirit and soul. That's why anyone can be a witch no matter if they are missing body parts or lack sensation. Their spirit feels it. Their spirit is grounded."

I also talked to a young woman at a recent festival. I first complimented her on her sandals and then noticed one of her feet was prosthetic. I asked her about grounding. She replied that she'd had the foot for most of her life and when she grounded, she pulled energy in with both of her feet. She didn't notice which was which—they are both her feet.

Minerals are believed to be aids in getting grounded, of earthing, which is another way to say the same thing. Holding agate, jade, bloodstone, hematite, and some other minerals seems to help some people with grounding, while amethyst seems to be the go-to for almost everything these days. You can easily find a string of these stones at most rock shops and metaphysical stores to wear around your neck or wrist to aid in grounding. I would use gravel, the heart of the mountain, if needed. I have suggested placing a little soil in the shoes and in the pocket when grounding feels impossible.

Finding Your Grounding Method

I can't stress enough how important it is to find a grounding protocol that works for you. Far too many people dismiss it with a wave of the hand—probably because they haven't found a way that satisfies them. Once you have felt the strength and stability that flows into your body from an effective grounding technique, you will never look back.

At festivals and conferences, it is so satisfying to watch the energy shift when I ask the observers to ground. Some people do that so easily that they don't have much technique to talk about. I see them subtly wiggle and their spines stretch out and straighten. Others have elaborate rituals and visualizations that get them to that deeply connected place.

However, some attendees will shake their heads and talk about how they used to be really good at it, but lately it has failed them. I was fascinated to hear that. Usually a technique, once mastered, is honed to a fine point through much use. Yet they've tried different techniques, but nothing feels as effective as it used to.

It's as if—as many have articulated—the energetic core of the planet is no longer solid. Imagine hearing that again and again all over this country and in places in Britain and Europe. The explanation goes something like this: I set deep roots and begin to feel connected, when there's a ripple and I lose contact. It is difficult and sometimes impossible to regain the strong connection. Any subsequent link feels tenuous and spotty.

Because of such reports, I decided to explore another style of grounding that seems to work for some folks and does work for me most of the time. I share it here for your consideration, especially if you have experienced what I've outlined.

The Lady and the Hawk

Imagine yourself a muscular young hawk, sitting on the gloved hand of the earth as Gaia. You dig your talons into the familiar glove, know the familiar smells and sights and sounds of being a trained raptor on the arm of a goddess. Shake your bells. Flex your wings. Solid, solid connection.

And then the leather-clad arm shifts, lowers, and then raises. You gather your wings to you and bend your knees, flexing your talons and releasing your grip. As the arm raises into the wildness of the sky, you lift off, with a thrust of your powerful wings and a lifting and then—you're away. You can return when you choose but are not as bound as you once were. If you are having trouble with grounding, try this protocol and see if it helps.

Explore Many Methods

The practice of grounding can take many forms, and it is worth your while to explore as many as you need to find the ones that work for you. When you have found one that feels right—and, more importantly, that is effective—use it as needed and practice it so that it is swift and sure. Since much of grounding is about your mood and situation, the protocol you have chosen and spent time perfecting may not always work. You may find yourself chafing against it, and that is not unusual. Just as your hair stylist suggests that you switch shampoos for best effect, you will also find that sometimes you need to do something else to stay effective. Try a different way and use that for a while. Having several strong techniques at your fingertips gives you an advantage that will serve you well.

In the relative peace of my home and land, I find that my preferred technique works well. But at a festival in an unfamiliar place, I may choose a different style of grounding. If I'm in a large and vibrant city at a new conference, I tend to use a different technique. Having all these tools in your workbasket allows you flexibility and security.

Into Your Burrow for Healing and Safety

In addition to using a grounding technique to strengthen and stabilize, we can look at grounding as a place of rest and healing. In this frenetic and overbooked world it is important to remember what all animals know: sometimes we all need to get in our burrow and seek shelter. Those of us who loved Kenneth Grahame's *The Wind in the Willows*, A. A. Milne's tales of Winnie-the-Pooh and friends, or Beatrix Potter's charming anthropomorphic characters have a fanciful idea of what a well-appointed burrow looks like. Likewise, if you are an observer of nature, you have a good idea of how dry, warm, and cozy real animal dens are, even without the curtains and Edwardian furniture.

Where You Can Go

When your soul and your body need to stop and rest, create a safe and comfortable place to retire to. Pick a visualization that suits you, whether you are a fan of fat teapots or a bed of dry leaves, and make that your spiritual den, your own private burrow. When anxiety, fear, or insecurity is overwhelming, go to this imagined place through visualization, go to ground like a small furry animal.

When you decide on this visualization, you can build activities into it, activities that are restorative. Some will be literal (like eating something special or creating a craft object that you enjoy) and others will grow in your imagination, in your mind's eye.

Nesting

One of the most often used items on my home altar is a woven basket shaped like a deep nest. It has a bit of soft padding in the bottom and various items have inhabited it from time to time. It is a safe space for my ragged soul to perch or to dive into, and I sometimes invite others' equally ragged souls to enjoy that quiet space. This is a variation on the idea of burrowing that is especially helpful for those of us who are ill at ease in confined spaces. The open top encourages a sense of safety with the additional comfort of being able to see out, metaphorically speaking.

Food

Ingesting certain foods is a definite aid in the grounding process. Even the act of chewing can bring us back to awareness of our physical selves. If you are having trouble getting yourself into a grounded headspace, consider for a moment when you last ate. If it was several hours before, the jitters you are feeling may not be energetic but physical. After a session of meditation (and certainly after trance work), it is important to get your energetic self firmly reconnected to your physical self. The recommendations outlined here are subject to your personal dietary choices and restrictions and are offered as examples only. If you have an allergy or sensitivity to particular foods or don't eat them for whatever reasons, there are plenty of other good grounding choices. You should never ingest something that you know discomforts your body.

Chocolate is one of my first choices, the darker the better. It's best to avoid sugar-rich foods because they often have the opposite of the desired effect. Initially, you will get a buzz from the sugar, but a crash happens soon after. A sugar crash is just that—a crash of mood and energy that makes grounding more difficult because you are at a low ebb.

Root vegetables, cooked or raw, are also good to get into your belly. Raw carrots, radishes, and beets and cooked potatoes, sweet potatoes, yams, turnips, and onions are delicious and nutritious ways to achieve the desired outcome. These are not quick choices, though. But the act of preparing these veggies and roasting them will also help bring you solidly into your self.

An apple, an oatmeal cookie, and a spoonful of peanut butter all have the potential to do this work. Warm teas and bone broth will help your soul be at home in your body again. Alcohol and most psychoactives generally have the opposite effect than the one we are working to achieve. It is very helpful after engaging in those things to have some grounding foods—and lots of good hydration.

Crafting

If idle hands are the devil's workshop, then crafty and creative hands may be exactly the opposite. I find that the occasional bout of repetitive craft work is not only necessary but calming and grounding. Last night I took out five skeins of woolen yarns and rolled them into useful balls for future knitting projects. It required a little concentration to avoid annoying tangles but was basically a meditative act of unrolling the skein and rolling it into a ball. If you are a craft-oriented person, you'll have your own repetitive chores and can use them to help you feel grounded.

A *Thunder Shirt for Your Soul*

It is hardly surprising that we take better care of our companion animals than we do ourselves. They often eat fresher and healthier food, take walks, and get their toenails trimmed as needed. A recent development in animal care is a thunder shirt, a weighted, close-fitting vest that anxious dogs can wear during thunderstorms and fireworks holidays. The weight seems to comfort them in the same way some babies prefer to be wrapped loosely in a blanket, a practice called swaddling. My daughter preferred that and still does. She sleeps under a weighted blanket, which has the same effect.

You don't necessarily need a thunder shirt or weighted blanket, but having a favorite garment that is comfortable and holds good memories is another grounding tool you can make use of. I have a warm and ragged scarf that I sometimes wear when I want to be careful of what I say or when I feel that my words may make me vulnerable (it's around my throat for a reason). When we have something difficult to say—when the best course of action is to speak truth to power—a favorite scarf or necklace can ground us and settle us into the job of work we've chosen. We'll look at the hows and whys of protection magic (chapter 8) and glamoury (chapter 10) later in the book.

You may have a comfy shirt or vest that works for you in the same way and is easily donned in getting ready for a job of work or when you feel wobbly. Most of us have beloved garments that will serve very well.

Going to Water

It may seem like a strange idea to practice grounding by associating with water, but it is another potential trick to improve your ability to get grounded, to connect with the living earth. Standing by the side of a great river brings us the comparison of how the water flows versus our place as literal bystanders. It is sometimes easier to feel how bound we are to the place we stand when we contrast it with the perpetual movement of the waters. The same is true of smaller creeks and streams, as well as the vastness of the ocean or a large lake. The movement of the waters can lull us into our own sense of stability.

It may seem contraindicated to consider grounding with something as mutable as water—and it doesn't work for everyone. But it is another technique for you to explore as you are finding what works best for you; it is another way to get yourself into a place of stability where you can do your work.

Many Native American peoples have a spiritual practice called "going to water." It is a way of connecting with Spirit in prayer, expressing gratitude for life and family. It is a place of healing as well as thanksgiving. The very act of going to water also constitutes grounding and focusing techniques.

Native American peoples are not the only ones that find their way to water on a regular basis as a spiritual activity. Baptism is one of the sacraments in the Christian Church and involves everything from a sprinkle of water at a cistern (called a font) within the walls of the church up to a full immersion in a body of living water. The intention is to wash away perceived sin and make the person acceptable as a member of the church community, grounded in the tenets of the particular denomination. Not unlike a Cherokee woman going to water in gratitude, searching for healing and renewing her connection with the elements.

The cultural traditions that are legacies of my ancestors from Western Europe, the British Isles, and Ireland also indicate a reverence for water, especially its sources—the places where it springs from the earth. Some folk practices have continued for centuries and generations down to the present day. Two of these are well-dressing and hanging clouties at springs believed to be particularly strong or blessed.

Well-dressing is the result of a community's reverence for a local source of pure water. These water sources were and are understood to house benevolent spirit-beings. The remarkable gift of water springing from a cleft stone or the roots of a tree has always been a subject of celebration and gratitude to the people who benefit from this necessary element flowing freely into the upper world in which we live. The idea that it would be soiled or misused in any way would have seemed horrific to our ancestors. It was not only polluting and rendering unusable a practical resource, but it was also insulting the spirits of a holy place, potentially powerful spirits who could exact punishment for such sacrilege. One of the signs of a culture's decline is the neglect or abuse of the water that sustains us.

Seasonal celebrations that mark the turning of the year's wheel are punctuated with folkloric customs, including dressing the holy well. They occur at different times of the year when communities come together to honor the spirit of the place by adorning the springheads of their local holy wells with floral displays. These decorations harken back to those pagan times when the spirits inhabiting the water and the area around it were honored, fed, and sometimes appeased. This also happens at the source of a locally important stream or river, which is also the place where water forces its way to the surface and flows outward from that source. Holy springs are often centers for community healing and bonding and often function as a place of communal prayer. Clouties (or sometimes "clooties") are strips of fabric that are used as prayer ties, petitions hung over sacred waters for relief of suffering.

Standing firmly on the ground and observing the movement of water can be helpful in developing a sense of grounding, of wrapping spirit self snugly around physical self.

A Grounding and Comforting Meditation

I find guided meditations helpful, and I offer one here. Your successful practice of magic does not depend on your ability to follow a guided meditation, nor does an effective meditation journey assure you of some special connection to anything other than yourself. I have found them helpful in times when I've felt disconnected from my source of grounding or when my self-talk has become unhelpful or hurtful. We all experience these times—it is a part of living in a changing world and functioning in uncertain times. No matter how good your grounding technique, you will find that there are times when you are adrift or unbalanced. Sometimes these pass after you have done that despised chore or met a scary situation head-on. But if you find yourself more wobbly than usual and for a longer time than you remember, spending the time to reorient yourself is time well spent.

It is often helpful to have a soothing beverage nearby and to wear comfortable clothes. Reading a guided meditation is not the best format, so recording this on your phone, computer, or recording device will make it easier to follow. If you don't like the sound of your own voice, ask a beloved friend to record it for you.

Let's begin.

You are sitting in your favorite chair in your favorite place. The place is restful, and simply being there brings you a sense of deep peace. Begin by breathing slowly and deeply and acknowledging that you are taking this brief time to regroup and realign yourself because you deserve the same respect that you have given others, as well as the same love you easily bestow on those you cherish. Throughout the meditation, bring your thoughts back to your breathing and adjust if you are no longer breathing deeply, slowly, and evenly. There will be notes here, along the way, to help you do so.

Feel the chair upholding you, welcoming you to rest completely in its support. Your attention is claimed by a movement at the window nearest you and you turn to observe a small bird eating seeds. In your mind's eye, you rise and walk to the window to watch the lovely bird. When it flies away, you walk to the door and open it, to see where the bird has gone. Carefully close the door behind you and turn to face the road before you.

Tend to your breathing.

The path from the door takes you to a dirt road, and you follow the path to the road. The bird is in the hedge ahead of you and takes flight the moment your feet are on that stony road. Feel the way your body adjusts to the uneven surface of the road. The bird flies from shrub to shrub along the hedgerow and you follow at a comfortable pace. The hills rise just ahead of you and the roadway winds toward the hedgerow and then away, repeating that pattern as you approach those old, low hills.

Tend your breathing and take a drink if you feel the need or desire to do so.

The bird alights on a steep bank in the foothills of the mountains, and you observe a spring of bright water cascading from a rock face, the wet stone luminescent. You approach the waterfall slowly, aware that this place holds meaning for you, holds healing for you. The water falls into a natural basin that has been enhanced by smooth stones placed by loving and respectful hands. You kneel beside the basin and look at its mottled surface, seeking your reflection. See your face there, as you are right now. What are you wearing? What is your expression? Touch the water with the flat palm of your hand. It is cool to the touch and invigorating. You raise your hand to your lips and touch your tongue to the water drops it holds. Relish the coolness of it and the fresh sweetness of the water's taste.

Now tend your breathing for a moment.

Return your gaze to the surface of the water and begin to notice the depth of the pool in front of you. It seems to be bottomless, and you see a light in the depths of the water. Without hesitation, you slip into the water and dive toward the light. You soon come out on a beachfront, and you wade onto the sand. The water surrounds you on all sides and murmurs to you, welcomes you. You sit down on the soft surface and then recline, feeling the warm sand beneath you and the sweet breeze on your face.

Breathe.

With your eyes closed, you hear soft footsteps approach you and feel a being crouching at your side. You stretch out your hand and it is taken by your companion. Your eyes remain closed. You are secure, safe, comfortable. With your back pressed into the sand and your hand gently but firmly held by your companion, you begin to feel the grounding effect of the sand, the murmuring waters all around you. You feel the warmth of the sand begin to energize your body and you drink it in, storing it in the energetic battery inside your body. Your companion lifts your hand, and you rise slowly from your prone position to a sitting one and from there to standing. You feel your companion leaving your side and hear a gentle splash as that being returns to the water. You are deeply grounded now, at one with the elements of earth and water. You step to the water's edge and discover the twin of the basin in the foothills. Tend to your breathing now and have a sip of your drink.

You again place your palm on the water and touch your fingers to your lips. Then, as before, you look at your reflection and see beyond it a light in the bottom of the pool. Diving in, you come quickly out of the water and step from the basin onto the grass. You note the cascade on the rock face and see the little bird waiting for you in the hedgerow. You and the bird return the way you came, down the winding dirt road until you come to the path that takes you back to your comfortable chair. You open the door and step inside, closing the door behind you. You return to that delicious chair and sit down, observing that the bird is once more eating seeds on the ledge of the window.

You check your breathing and your grounding. Placing your hands on the tops of your thighs, you come fully back to your physical self. You are calm, grounded, and safe. You and the spirit of the sacred well have understood each other and been in communion. You may always make this journey when your soul is thirsting for grounding and the companionship of the spirits of the sacred well.

Under the Sky

As we continue exploring the possibilities for deepest connection and grounding, stand with me for a moment under the sky. Whether yours is a sliver between buildings, runs from ridgetop to ridgetop, or expands itself to the horizons on all sides, the great vault of the sky has always been a significant partner in the practice of magic. It isn't all *Sturm und Drang* like Modest Mussorgsky's (and Disney's) *Night on Bald Mountain*. Often it is a gentle place of moving clouds and birds. It can cover our heads like a cloak's hood or leave us cowering under the threat of storm and wind.

In either case the sky forms a barrier for us through that tricky gravity. As we gaze up at the sky, we can notice how firmly our feet press into the soil. The dome above us reminds us of the solid girth of the land beneath us, reminds us of our earthy selves. When you are experimenting with grounding techniques that will work for you consistently, try standing under the sky and feeling your bonding with the planet. Sometimes that reminder is all our souls need to feel the connection and be comforted and supported by it.

Day Sky

Dawn and dusk are liminal times when change is visible, palpable. As a priestess, these are the times I choose when doing "prayers for the world," as I sometimes do in times of collective grief and shock. As a witch, I feel out these times for their supportive power in particular workings. Living in a mountain region, it is easy to observe the sun seemingly slipping over the edge of the western hills, adding startling bands of color to the darkening sky. Dawning here is more subtle but no less powerful, as the darkness yields to a sun unseen but still brightening the world. The absence of color—the stark grayness—gives way slowly. When the sun's rays finally rip through the oak and maple trees to the east of the house, they hold a glaring revelation of light, of promise.

When we speak in general terms of waxing and waning, we can apply that to the movement of the planet around the sun. Sunset is a time to release, to bind, and to cover over. The sun's rising lends uplift, newness, and uncovering. Both are times of supportive power, and the experienced witch will find the inherent worth of these gifts and will use them well.

Night Sky

One of the many benefits of traveling is the opportunity to stand on different land, to explore different natural systems. I've spent most of my life in the southern highlands of the Appalachian Mountains—a land with slow, long pulses of life-force energy with thin soil, small but dangerous rivers, and ever-present trees and greenness. Not every land is like the land with which I live. Not every land has the trees that are here (and some have none).

I always look for the familiar healthful plants and am always confused when there is no mugwort, no rabbit tobacco. In these new-to-me lands, I always begin with grounding, with testing my roots in unfamiliar soil. Then I look up.

The skies are as varied as the land bases under our feet. We have a narrow belt of sky here because we live in the bottom of a cup that is made of mountains. The sun has long risen, and the gardens are bright long before we see the sun. The sun sets behind the western mountains and that is that. We know the planet is still turning, but even if we went beyond that range of hills, we'd only find another range of hills, and so on until we reach somewhere in Tennessee. The Blue Ridge might better be called the Blue Ridges, hill after hill, disappearing into the horizon.

I also live on the edges of a small town and my street was given bright streetlights as an aid to the gentrification of this working-class community. This means that we see the day sky for a limited number of hours because of the mountains and we see the night sky only by looking away from the lights and focusing our eyes on the western sky.

But the Midwest is different—and I've been spending time there in recent years, often camping under that broad sky. Certainly the land is different and a little disconcerting for a mountain person, but seeing so much of it—day or night—is astounding and awe-inspiring. So much sky, so much to observe and ponder.

The night sky seems not only bigger but somehow closer. I rejoice to see the celestial mist that is the Milky Way stretching above and away from me in all directions. An October moon rising in the flatlands of Kansas is a fierce and orange wonder of light and … presence.

I haven't spent much time in the Southwest, but an invitation to an interfaith gathering in Salt Lake City gave me the gift of meeting several Ute people and touching both the land and the sky there. A family visit to Las Vegas afforded me a little more time there, this time in the desert. It's hardly possible to imagine a place more opposite to the one I live in and yet it was full of life and beauty. I finally understood what people meant about "the light" there and know why so many people are drawn to arid and powerful places. To stand on a mesa with the light-world above and the stone-world below is to know your place, to touch a strange link to eternity.

What does all this have to do with grounding? How can we alter our usual grounding methods by grounding to the sky? We are exploring so many ways to ground, to get ready to do magic, and the sky above offers us another way.

I often tie specific prayers and workings to that wonderfully liminal time when the sun creeps below the western skyline. In the gloaming, at twilight, there is a special feeling that takes us out of the day-to-day and into a time out of time. We have to move somewhat quickly because there is no stopping the schedule of sundown to night.

Take yourself outside and stand under the sky where you are. Simply stand there, listening, observing. Search the limits of the sky that is your sky. Note the color, the placement of sun or moon, the presence or absence of clouds. Let your gaze rest on the horizon, however close or faraway it seems. As you observe the vast expanse above you, you may find that you feel very earthy and quite small. That feeling can help you snuggle up to the land under your feet and give you the sense of being connected to the place on which you stand.

The night sky is a wonder that never ceases to make me feel small but also connected in both directions, both below my feet and over my head. Creating a grounding protocol like a lifeline from the top of your head to the bottoms of your feet sets you in a place from which the deepest connections can be achieved.

The Importance of Paying Attention

Our species relies so much on our visual acuity, but we have other senses that also give us detailed information on the world around us. In learning to navigate the physical world as well as its non-physical counterparts, magic-workers need to strengthen as best they can all the natural senses. Most of us have one or two senses that are stronger, and all of us have senses that are compromised, either through incidents of genetics or through accidents and disease in our personal living history. The process of aging can also have an effect on the senses—we may find our eyesight weakening as we age, a process called presbyopia. Cataracts may form and, when corrected, people often mind their sight stronger than ever before. Aging may also affect hearing, sending us to professionals who can correct the problem (if we can afford for them to do so). Working to strengthen all our senses—smell, taste, touch, vision, and hearing—will go far in supporting us as we approach the other senses. As you are learning the ways of magic, be smart and pull to yourself the resources you need to be successful—one of those resources is sharpening your attention to the world around you.

I am saddened when people tell me they are too spacey, busy, or "airy" to know what's going on around them in the natural world. If that is your feeling, I encourage you to stop, to look, to listen. There is so much to learn by paying attention, not only to the people around you, but to the weather, the land, and the spirit that surrounds you. I come from a land where traditional farmers are expert weather predictors and midwives know how close a woman is to birthing by the smells and sounds in the birthing room. Several years back, a group of New Age healers gathered in a local park to encourage others to help them create a healing event. We stood in a circle and listened to the details of the idea. I was standing between two herbalists and heard them muttering under their breath, cataloguing the healthful herbs that were growing at our feet. We counted fifteen plants that were common and readily available. The organizers barely acknowledged the land around and under them. It was revealing about their intentions, but it made me a little sad.

I hope you are seeing all the variations for a sense of security— of integration of soul and body—to make your life as a magic-worker grounded as well as flexible. Some of these protocols can be done quickly as part of your preparation to work or when you are feeling overwhelmed by circumstances. But some of them are ongoing practices that can be incorporated into your regular practice that can be stored in our bodies for later, as we store energy.

One of them will work for you. It may take you several tries to find the right one, but it is worth the effort and time it takes to master it. From a deeply grounded place, you not only gather your focus and gain strength and confidence. You also open the channels to pull energy from the earth and elsewhere to use in your work.

NOW YOU TRY

There are so many people having trouble getting grounded and enjoying the energy that comes from doing this easily. This chapter outlined several ways to get there. Some of the suggestions may have surprised you. Grounding to moving water or through observation of the sky may have offered you some new ideas about stabilizing your body and wrapping your physical and spirit selves into a beautiful whole.

What is your favorite technique in this chapter? Try it for seven days and see how it works for you. If it doesn't, try something completely different.

> Hint: Remember, it's okay to try more than one until you find the one that fits best.

Chapter 7

Energy and Execution

*E*nergy. I use this word in so many classes and in so much of my writing. It was part of my vocabulary as an actor and a director and is one of the primal elements in the practice of magic. It is a shorthand word, though, isn't it? When I say *energy*, do I mean the same thing you are thinking when you hear that word? And how do you know that? It is one of the things I want to be clear about as we move forward. We will look at synonyms for the word and try to eke out a workable definition. When we have scratched around our complex language, we will do our best to scrape up something comprehensive and useable. Energy feels easily understood, and in our "simple, practical" way, it can be. But let's take a little time to wiggle through the idea of energy and see if we can find a definition that suits the work and isn't tricky to understand.

We use that word *energy* so much in discussing magical practice, as well as in our day-to-day lives, even in the ways we heat and light our homes. Let's take some time to look at that word, its various meanings, and the way it is used specifically in magic, which is sometimes called "energy work."

Energy equals mass multiplied by the speed of light squared. Isn't that what Einstein famously equationed? Potency. Power. Vitality. I spent some time with Einstein's theory and went down several physics rabbit holes. Energy as life force, as that material that is and powers the universe. When you've stayed up far too late and are facing the next day with a monumental sleep deficit, you may say that you're out of energy.

I shared a story from my interfaith days when each meeting started with a closed-eye moment of silence. These were uncomfortable for me, and I considered why that would be, then looked to nature for the answer. The natural world is almost never silent. Even in the cold of winter, there are scurrying sounds and the creak of tree branches in the wind. Night brings the sounds of owls, of foxes, of distant coyotes. I was being asked to close my eyes in a room filled with people who didn't understand my spiritual traditions and were uneasy with the word *witch*. In that silent place, full of unease, I was asked to close my eyes and be very vulnerable. This doesn't lead to comfortable camaraderie.

I suggested an alternative: What if we try beginning the meeting with a moment of rhythm? We started with a heartbeat—slapping our hands against our thighs. We observed each other, smiling at the sounds and the way our bodies began to move with the rhythm. This start gave us a chance for expression, an expression that was shared. It helped us connect as a network, like a web.

A Web of Energy

I have had many fruitful discussions in recent months about the mycelium network. If you are not familiar with the astounding work of Paul Stamets, please take the time to read *Mycelium Running* and ponder how the concept of a global network of interlacing mycelium changes your view of the interconnectedness of all things—a concept we also discuss at length and have done in the West for quite a while.

This morning I sat down with my apprentice and friend Amanda, someone with whom I discuss batty ideas about being a modern animist in the world. This morning we talked about mycelium and the strange network that we are noticing at long last and what that system means to the planet. We looked at other connected systems—air (molecules), tree roots and mother trees, mycelium networks. Illustrating with my outstretched fingers, I suggested that these networks are not only alive, but they are also working, constantly moving energy back and forth. I touched my fingertips to each other and pressed the ends of my fingers together. It's not only that the seeking cords meet and connect but that the connection of the two energy sources then shoots energy back through the entire network, enlivening it through the connection's energetic transfer and enabling the other seeking cords to continue to seek—and find—new network connections. The energy continues to flow and build as the network pulses with life.

I used the example of effective politicians and preachers and the way that they—whether consciously or subconsciously—use energy. There are two interesting practices that inhabit much of the fanciful ideas of the region of southern Appalachia: snake handling and speaking in tongues. These practices, one of which is based on the interpretation of a Bible verse, are extraordinary to witness, but the handling of snakes is now, blessedly, rare. The snakes are always stout and venomous—rippling copperheads, muscular diamondback rattlers. There is often rhythmic music as part of this worship practice, and that rhythm is an important aspect. The handlers mimic it, the congregation feels it, the snakes settle into it, and because of this energy that fills the small church, the snakes are usually handled with care and without striking. The energy of that rhythm lulls all present into a synchronous space, together in this act of worship, just as it had with that interfaith group.

Speaking in tongues sometimes accompanies this event. Speaking in tongues is believed to be an ability that falls on the faithful, allowing them to speak a language they don't know—the language of angels. When one congregant falls to this, it usually spreads throughout the congregation and is an exultation of worship, appreciated and beloved.

At the height of his power and influence, Bill Clinton had an extraordinary way of moving energy. A packed auditorium is waiting for him to appear. The energy is high. He steps behind the lectern to great applause and sounds of welcome. He draws that energy in and returns most of it to the audience through gestures and verbal signals. The audience energy sustains, grows higher and denser, and then returns to the man at the lectern. He takes in half and returns half to them. This continues throughout his speech, which is why he could speak literally for hours at a time. You can see this in successful preachers and other performers, which is why they often seem indefatigable.

"Low Vibing"

There is much talk in many communities about so-called negative energy and "low vibing." When teaching, I often laugh about the many crystals, herbs, and so forth that will eliminate negative energy and allow one to live a blissful life of positive revitalization through this corrected energy. This notion is part of the overpowering, bright-siding crowd that is seemingly incapable of dealing with much of life without lots of light and love. I use this example when teaching about energy and its uses and sources. The energy that toasts your bread in the morning so that you may have toast and marmalade is the same energy that will toast your ass if you stick the butter knife into a plug. The energy is the same. It is the usage that determines the outcome. This force we call energy is not dependent on the practitioner's mood or the mood of the magic-worker's immediate surroundings or the mood of the times, the zeitgeist.

When I am asked to do an in-home visit because someone in the house has determined that there is spirit manifestation present, I am never surprised to learn that the person who called me is responsible for generating the overload of energy. Do you remember that old fairy tale "Why the Sea Is Salt," in which careless words caused the salt grinder to continually grind until, in fear and frustration, the owner throws it into the sea? Or the modern children's book with the sensible—and adorable—village witch called Strega Nona? She has a magic pasta pot that happily cooks up the right amount of supper because Strega Nona knows both the words to command it to cook and the words to cease the cooking. When her assistant, Big Anthony, decides to make pasta while Strega Nona is away from home, he succeeds in getting the supper to happen but doesn't know the words to make the pasta pot stop cooking. Strega Nona returns to find a predictable river of pasta and knows exactly what has happened.

It can happen to the people in our lives, this surfeit of vitality, of energy. The person who contacts me about the house is often flooding the place with their own ceaseless energy which, in turn, gets bunged up in the corners of the rooms and bumps around until it is encouraged to flow into the center of the living space and from there go out the doors or windows. I will then do the work of encouraging the occupant to do their own clearing by sweeping through the house with a broom, moving from front door to back and getting in all the corners. It almost always helps.

In the discussion of what is energy, Amanda and I went through the energy gathering protocol that I learned long ago and still practice. After intentional grounding with tiny roots coming out through the bottoms of the feet, the energy worker pulls energy up into the body to center in the belly battery. We both practiced that and then wondered at all the things those spirit roots encounter on their way—the geological history of the planet itself, the traumas, and adventures from the very beginning of the planet itself. At last, we come to the molten iron core that energizes the planet itself, regardless of the flora, fauna, and fungi that occupy the surface and the below-ground portions that can sustain life. Neither of us knew about the moon and whether or not it had a core, so we pulled out our phones and the NASA website gave us the fascinating answer: the moon has a solid core, surrounded by a molten core, both of which are mostly iron. Like human blood, like rust, like the native Appalachian red clay. We are connecting iron to iron, from our blood to the planet's core, from our blood to the moon's core. It makes our ideas of connective energies seem even more compelling and important.

If you are curious about the spiritual composition of the land beneath your feet, I heartily recommend that you use one of your practice sessions to explore. Ground yourself using one of the methods that weaves your spirit into the planet, like the one with little roots wiggling down. Once you feel dug in, tend to your breathing. What are you sensing from those roots? Before you start harvesting energy, consider what's in there. How might those minerals and memories impact your workings? How can you use them to best advantage? How can you begin to heal the wounds of those memories? There is much to consider in all those layers below our questioning feet.

Energy Harvesting

All of us carry around energy, and it is one of the things that enable us to do our work and live our lives. It is our life force. We need to be resourceful about acquiring as well as using energy because we don't want to tap that juicy life force without good cause. Many practitioners disagree with me about this theory, but I fervently believe—and just as fervently practice—that you are foolish to use your own, finite, life force in the practice of magic. Why would you when there are easily tapped sources all around you, at all times? The short answer is you wouldn't unless you were unaware of these other sources or untrained in acquiring and using them.

I'm going to share some of my favorite energy sources and, as always, I ask that you try some of them and see if they work for you.

Earth: The easiest for me, for whatever reason, is to draw energy from Earth herself. It is a planet that is revolving as well as orbiting the sun, so the action of that brings wind and weather and all sorts of helpful sources for retrieving energy. It is also a good place to leave any excess energy you have harvested and for which you don't have a current use—I bend and place my flat palms on the soil and release it into that soil through my hands. You will know you have an excess of harvested energy when you start to feel a little wobbly, shaky. (Also take a moment to consider the last time you ate or drank water. Those deficits can cause shakiness too.) Wind and storm are also excellent sources of earth-based energy.

Sun: Good ol' Sol, our nearest and dearest star, flows energy over our planet all the time. Two things to be aware of are the relative distance from Earth to the sun and the tilt of the planet away from the sun. These will vary the amount of energy somewhat but never enough to matter. Please be mindful of solar flares too, when the fiery surface of the sun expels bright arcs of energy. Try harvesting some of those and schedule special workings for those times. You will feel an extra jolt of power that can be used to achieve a magical goal.

Moon: Lunar energy is the kind most associated with this work we do. We all can imagine a group of magic-workers under the light of a fat and full moon. But each phase brings its own style of energy, which we'll discuss in a moment.

Free Radical: *Free radical* is my silly name for the energy that appears quickly—and usually loudly—and disappears with the same speed. (Actual free radicals are unstable molecules that are missing electrons from their outer shell.) These include sirens, cars with insufficient mufflers, loud arguments, boisterous children, and train horns blown as a warning at level-grade crossings. This energy is free for the taking and doubles as a way to temper your annoyance at disturbing sounds. Pull the energy into your battery and store it for later or return it to the earth.

Storing Energy

I was taught to store the energy I acquire in the center of my body, and you find that by putting the flat of your hand on your stomach with the bottom edge above your belly button. Go ahead and try that now. Easy. Rub your hands together and warm them through the friction, then place them on your belly in the energy storage place. Think of this as your physical battery. As we go through some of the ways to collect and harness energy, try to remember this strong container and celebrate it as an important tool.

Begin by grounding yourself in whichever way you've found best. If you've sent down little roots from the bottoms of your feet, you can use those roots to pull energy up from the planet. If you've found a different way to ground, do it now. From this sturdy place, press your feet down as firmly as you can. Feel the physical connection between your feet and the firm place below them.

For those of you with neuropathy or other conditions that limit the feeling in your feet, a guided meditation may help you achieve the same goals. Use your hands as a stand-in for your feet. Press them together or, when sitting, press them onto the tops of your thighs. The important thing is to put your physical self into intentional contact with the spiritual force of the planet, to connect in a meaningful and intentional way. From that point, allow the stresses and anxieties that you are carrying in your strong legs to flow down into the soil below your feet, energetically emptying your lower body (from your belly button downward) so that you can fill it with fuel for your work.

It sometimes helps our visualization to think of energies as colors. I was taught that in the beginning of my training and have found it to be useful all these years later. When I am accessing earth energies, I see them in my mind's eye as grass green. They flow up into my empty legs and into the battery in the middle of my body. After mastering this technique, you'll find yourself knowing when you've gathered enough to fill your bag-like legs and fill your battery.

If you are also planning to use celestial energies—the sun's, for instance—it may be your choice to fill your battery halfway and then reverse the process to gather energy from the sun. Once you are grounded and have filled the lower half of your body with green, imagine that the top of your head opens to receive the sky energy. Let the anxieties, stresses, and obstacles to your work float up out of the top of your head, emptying your upper body in preparation to receive the sun's bounty. Once you are empty, allow it to flow into you and over you, filling your battery and upper body with sunlight and energy. You may feel it swirling into the green already in your battery and combining to become one clear energy stream.

Using the Power of the Moon

You now see how many sources of energy are available to a witch to power her life and her work. Despite all these sources, much folklore pairs witches with the moon and the moonlight. Witches are believed to spend all our time in the night-land, either under a fat full moon or a sliver of a crescent newly revealed, doing dark deeds under cover. But we know that much of our work happens in broad daylight walking in the workaday world.

Let's take a moment to visit that night-land, where our alter egos dance around bone-fires and fly about on brooms. Let's abide in that place that is—always—under the moon.

I recently learned a new descriptor for human techniques for working with the phases of the moon. It is *moon mapping* and I like that—it appeals to my inner cartographer. That phrase usually refers to how we can improve our health and our moods by staying in touch with the moon, but we are looking for a different kind of mapping, as we explore all the sources of our power and useable energy.

There are traditional uses for lunar energy, and I sometimes use those. But in the years of practicing, I have discovered other ways of working with the power of the moon, and I will share those too. I realized there was an issue for me when I noted that most people are restless—and often sleepless—under a full moon, but I react in the opposite way. I sleep deeply during the days of the full moon. I love being situated so that the full moon can shine upon me while I sleep. But when the dark and new moon come around, I am restive and uneasy.

Why We Have Moon Phases

Here are the traditional moon phases: new, waxing crescent, first quarter, waxing gibbous, full, waning gibbous, last quarter, waning crescent, and dark.

Obviously, over the course of a month, no portion of the moon ever leaves the sky. Just as we insist on continuing to say "the sun rises" and "the setting of the sun" long after we are aware that the sun doesn't move at all. It is we who spin and orbit, easy in our planetary dance around our star. We have phases of the moon because of the way the bodies move around each other. The bit we see illuminated is reflecting the light of our close star.

How do you tell if it's waxing or waning? Think DOC.

If the shape of the crescent forms the bulb-out part of a capital D, the moon is waxing to full—the O. If the crescent makes the shape of a C, it is waning to a dark moon and then to new. What we see in the night sky is the part of the moon that is lit by the light of the sun.

It is easy to remember DOC and to trace the direction of the bump with the curve of your hand held to the crescent moon in the sky.

The feel of the energy from each phase varies from person to person, so if the following paragraphs don't mirror your experience, that is perfectly fine. What I perceive happening across my shoulders, you may sense in your toes, just as our taste buds sense flavors differently, which is why some people love foods with cilantro while others think it tastes like soap. One person loves cream in her coffee, but her best friend finds that disgusting. Dark chocolate is the delight of many, while others find it too strong and bitter, preferring milk chocolate. The trick is for us to differentiate for ourselves how the phases affect us so that we can use them effectively in our magical workings. And, just as our taste for a certain food may change over time, you may find that you sense the touch of the phases differently as you mature or as your life situation changes.

New Moon, Dark Moon

Some people don't differentiate between dark moon and new moon, but I was taught a little differently. Here's how I treat these differences and the way that works for me. Back in the day, we took up the idea that dark moon is the time in which no moon can be seen in the sky—not the tiniest sliver—and was a time of intense power, a time when the moon, like a fine sauce, had been reduced to its richest and most effective essence. Under the hidden face of the dark side of the moon, we may delve into hollow places, into forbidden places, into nooks and crannies of a different sort of authority and experience. The waves of this moon phase often strike us in the profound inner workings of our pelvic areas—you can feel it there, latent, waiting, strong as stone.

First Quarter

A day or so later, that precious crescent appears like a promise, and that energy feels quite different from the dark moon. It is waxing into fullness, and the energy can feel somewhat tentative until we reach the first quarter. It hits us higher in our bodies, working up the spine, uncoiling and rippling as it rises.

Waxing Gibbous

After the first quarter, the moon is a waxing gibbous moon. *Gibbous* means "swollen" or "humpbacked" and comes from the Latin *gibbus*, which means "hump" (like the one on a camel). We are visually nearer full moon now, and you may feel this phase rolling up and down from toes to throat and back again, preparing us for those last few days before full moon. It can be an energizing time—for some, maybe too energizing. If you know this phase has such an effect on you, you may choose to mark your calendar and choose workings that require this galloping intensity.

Full Moon

There it is, hanging broad and bright in the sky—full moon. It seems to beam down on us, and children the world over form intense bonds to this phase. Folklore is filled with stories about this phase too—our eyes invite us to tell stories of what seems pictured in the shadows of the lunar landscape. Some say a rabbit or hare, some say a man with a bundle of sticks. Most of us can easily discern what looks like a smiling face on the wide surface. Shakespeare described it as a man with a thorn-bush in his A *Midsummer Night's Dream*.[1]

I have talked with colleagues from the Acjachemen Nation in California, where the women do not do energy work during the stasis of this phase but instead use it to refill their own energy storehouses. I feel the full moon as if I were standing under a slow waterfall and then wrapped in my favorite old cloak. It surrounds me and flows into me, bringing fullness to the empty places—physical, emotional, and spiritual. It is a healing bath of gentle moonlight in which I do my best to schedule no workings at all.

In some cultures, the full moon in a particular month or season has a name that reflects that time. Snow moon, blood moon, and worm moon are evocative ways to speak of this little satellite that we hold so dear. It also holds much on Earth in its sway—as well as humans and other animals being affected by the moon—the tides in oceans and great lakes are affected by it. The gravitational pull of the moon (and the sun) is the cause.

Other Ways to Raise Energy for Harvesting

We have looked at ways of harvesting available energy, but it's also important to remember that this important resource can be produced through your own efforts. One of my favorites is through dancing. Please don't panic if you don't consider yourself a dancer. I'm not talking about a dance or movement performance. I'm talking about the full integration of body and soul, woven into a joyful whole and stepping into a space of ecstasy. You can do it with others or all by yourself. Even if you have two left feet, even if you've been told your entire life that you can't dance.

---

1. William Shakespeare, A *Midsummer Night's Dream: The Folger Shakespeare Library Edition* (New York: Simon and Schuster, 2004), act 5, scene 1, line 273.

Irish Stomping Dance

A Brigidine nun from Kildare Town in Ireland once taught a lively, simple stomping dance to a group of invited guests from the local community. We use it here to wake the earth at Imbolc and to stimulate the old dear at Beltane. Here's how you do it—and best with some drummers to help.

In a circle, we will move clockwise together. First, shift your weight to your left foot and with your right foot stomp the directions: north, east, south, west. Now shift your weight to your right foot and stomp the directions with your left foot: north, east, south, west. Shift your weight to be equally balanced on both feet. Then step to the left and bring your right foot to be by your left. Repeat that step, then return to the stomping part.

The call of the dance goes like this: "Ready. North, east, south, west. Shift. North, east, south, west. Step. Together. Step. Together." You may also choose to stomp with each foot. Change the call to "Ready. Stomp. Stomp. Stomp. Stomp ..." and so on. The late Bronwen Forbes's wonderful book *Make Merry in Step and Song: A Seasonal Treasury of Music, Mummer's Plays & Celebrations in the English Folk Tradition* is a terrific resource and is listed in the bibliography.

Most rituals I facilitate include a section of movement, and it is important to be as inclusive as possible. You can consider the requirements of elders and other people who may not be physically able to engage in movement. They are often asked to sit in the center, if they so desire, and hold that space. From there, they can experience the swirling and lively energy without risking their well-being.

Other Rhythmic Methods

In addition to dances of all sorts as tools to raise the energy level, there is also drumming, chant, and rhythmic clapping.

Drumming is a wondrous stimulant, whether you are the drummer, the dancer, or the listener. In many summer festivals, there is a designated area with a firepit and a covered area for drummers. Most people seem to play large African and African-style drums, with a few frame drummers. There is also a place with rattles, bells, and other rhythm instruments.

We carry musical instruments in our bodies too. Chant, song, and clapping our hands or striking our thighs are also delightful ways to raise and relish this energy. Try them at gatherings and don't be shy about trying any or all of them as you are revving yourself up in the morning.

Free Energy

We have explored many ways to acquire energy for our work, but one of my favorites is the concept of "free energy"—that vital linkage that doesn't require much effort to take in. The example that I often use involves fire trucks and ambulances. When a city's emergency response teams are activated—often through a phone call to a central dispatcher—the choice is sometimes made to send everyone possible. A fire truck, an ambulance, and a police car may arrive at the same house in response to the 911 call. They almost always come roaring in, lights flashing, sirens wailing. If it is your beloved grandmother on the floor with an unknown but debilitating condition, you will be glad of so much expertise. But if you are the neighbor up the street, all that noise and light and the pulse of those heavy vehicles speeding through your neighborhood may be disturbing or even triggering. As a magic-worker, you may choose to capture that free energy and use it for your own work. As we've discussed before, you ground yourself so you are able to receive the energy. Then you pull it into your body and center it in your battery zone.

When that battery in the center of your body is fully charged, it is useful for workings, certainly. But it is a handy place to replenish your own energy in times that are draining or difficult. We all have those times, and this backup storage is good for magic and good for life.

❧❧❧

NOW YOU TRY

As we see in this chapter, there are many ways to gather the energy you need without using your personal life force to do magic. Here's something to try: spend a month determining how the phases of the moon touch you and the following month checking to see if the first month's information was valid and useful.

Hint: Always do some relaxation and centering before you harvest energy. It makes it much easier.

Chapter 8

Protection and Pushback

As you become more familiar with the stepping stones of magical practice, you will understand that the distractions you may be experiencing can come from outside you and your practice area. In addition to your brain reviewing the list of all you have to do, there are distractions from your neighborhood, the other people and animals in your house, and traffic noises from outside. This chapter covers ideas for shielding and warding and will also look at possible defensive action. However, before you conclude that someone else is interfering with your work (many of us are quick to jump to conclusions about that), practice personal shielding to bring yourself to a place of clear discernment.

Embrace Fortunality

I want to begin with another foundational piece of good practice and of self-care as a magic-worker. It is a strong talisman to hold as you are focusing on invisible walls and energetic fields. It is luck. I love the word *fortunality*. Two friends were having a discussion on social media, and because it was social media, I was able to eavesdrop on the conversation and to join in at one point. I hardly remember what was being discussed but one of them mentioned the concept of fortunality and my ears pricked up.

Fortunality is the state of having good fortune. You can have good fortunality in the same way you have a good personality. You might be born with it, but it is certainly something that is developed throughout your life through accessing the tools to fill your personal world with good fortune, with good luck. We don't talk nearly enough about the place of luck—for good or ill—in modern cultures. It is one of those old-fashioned notions that were so important to our ancestors and one that colored their worldviews on many things. Folklore gives us so many ways to fix your luck and tales filled with examples of how a bout of good luck can change everything. There is a sense among us moderns that we make our own luck, and we often look down on those silly things one shouldn't do as it might affect one's luck, might be unlucky. A black cat crossing your path, walking under a ladder, opening an umbrella in the house. In my Appalachian culture, we have so many superstitious beliefs that we hold firm, never quite believing in the truth of it but also never willing to risk its possibility. My grandmother passed on to me her horror of placing shoes on a table or a hat on the bed, and I have tormented the people with whom I travel for years. No sooner has that fine summer hat been carefully removed from a suitcase and placed on a pillow than I am dashing for it like a rugby player, heaving myself onto the bed and holding the offending thing aloft, all while shrieking No! and lobbing it onto the nightstand.

There are talismans we can carry and gestures we can do to ward it off, this ill luck. I am a theater person, and the lengths we will go to avoid saying the name of the Scottish king in Shakespeare's

The Tragedy of Macbeth are remarkable. But the consequences of accidental speaking of that word or quoting lines from the play when not in rehearsal are elaborate indeed. I worked occasionally with a local Shakespeare-in-the-park group for several summers. One night as we were finishing rehearsals for a different play, a cast member asked about "the Scottish play" by its actual name, uttering the word *Macbeth* in the dressing room. The director and founder—a stickler for Shakespeare performed as it has come down to us, with no cuts or concepts—gasped aloud and in her deepest director voice intoned, "Get out!" The miscreant dawdled, not realizing how seriously she would take this breach in theater protocol. She grabbed him by the arm, hoisted him from a sitting position, and dragged him to the door, which she opened. She threw him out of the room and slammed the door behind him. The poor novice hadn't a clue what to do. One of the old-timers snuck out the shop area door and found the fellow staring at the closed door. He was informed that he had to spit over his left shoulder and walk around the theater three times, counterclockwise. When he arrived back at the door, he was to knock three times and then beg to be readmitted. At first he laughed, but the messenger was absolutely serious about what had to happen, and so the new actor complied. It doesn't seem too much to ask to ensure that the company and the current production would not be adversely affected by the storm of bad luck when it was so easily repelled.

This sort of elaborate methodology is common in many places—in shipyards and on boats, in professional kitchens, in bingo parlors. How many of us have a lucky talisman that we carry with us? Are you someone who finds four-leaf clovers, picks them, and saves them, pressed and taped onto a piece of stiff paper? We are saving up all those indicants, filling our luck bank against a time when we slip and do that unlucky thing that has been passed down to us through family or culture.

Claim Your Good Luck

That all seems like silliness to most people and something we do because it reminds us of family or of childhood. Unlike so many things we contemplate in the world of magic-making and witchery, repairing your luck is not the obvious first choice when something goes terribly wrong. We are looking at all the ways we can improve our skills, connect our intuition more firmly to our workaday lives, and be successful in this chosen work. If your first inclination when things go off the rails in your life is to blame someone else who has a grudge against you, you may be looking in the wrong place and should probably start with a ruthless examination of where you are, if and how you are practicing, and whether you have indulged in some habits that are not helpful in interpersonal relationships.

Then you would be wise to examine that luck bank and see if there are measures you can take to improve your luck. This requires you to understand that good fortune is indeed something that is needed to grease the wheels of life and to desire good luck for that purpose. All those little things you do "for luck" need to serve as the way you set your intention.

The first and easiest thing is to wake up every morning and claim your luck. As you brush your teeth or put on your shoes, declare to yourself that you are lucky, and that this day is going to be a fortunate one. Simple.

Charging a talisman is a valuable way to proceed too. Is there something you already consider a lucky charm? Charge it under a waxing moon and treat it as an important tool in your work. Keep it in your pocket, in your bag, or on your altar and acknowledge that it brings you something you need—added good fortune.

When we begin to treat good luck as a tool, we can discern how it is working in our lives. Mostly we don't know, to be honest. Your boss happens to see you doing a kindness and remembers that when it comes to a bonus or better position. You were in the right place at the right time, but you were also displaying your best nature, one that gains us brownie points with like-hearted people. But you may not perceive that as lucky but as a happy accident.

Sometimes we know when our luck is good because we narrowly escape disaster through no action of our own or we are present when the seemingly impossible occurs without warning. That was a lucky break. That was sheer luck. You can shine in the acknowledgment of the people who say about you that you are so lucky. Most of us know that luck is due mostly to persistence and hard work. But aiding those things, greasing the wheels of life, is another way to use intention as part of your skillset.

Shields Up

Your sacred self is worth protecting and that's what the meat of this chapter is concerning. There are two important techniques that with grounding and energy acquisition form the solid foundation of energy work and magic, and those are the protective pieces that we call shielding and warding. Shielding secures your personal boundaries and gives you a quiet space free from other people's energy and intentions. When we are adequately shielded, we can sit in a peaceful garden where we can think our own thoughts and feel our own feelings. It is a place set apart from and outside the physical world.

I will credit my enthusiastic but simplistic embrace of astrology for the opportunity to explore the protocols of shielding. I am a Pisces, with a Scorpio Moon. I am a typical Fish Sun—creative, intuitive, filled with mystical visions, and so easily hurt that it isn't even funny. I feel what those around me feel. It is a simplistic understanding to be sure, but it was a scary place to go through puberty and the first Saturn return. I read everything I could find about it (which wasn't much in the early 1970s) and found the best advice in a Sybil Leek book, *Diary of a Witch*. I can't remember the language she used, but I understood that sensitive people like me could create a wall around themselves so that they didn't have to feel all the complicated grown-up feelings that seemed to smother me. My first walls were made of the same material I knew all around me in the mountains, and I would spend time erecting in my imagination the barbed wire and wooden fences that kept the cows and horses in their pastures. Looking back, it was the sort of shielding I teach against today—permeable surfaces that aren't effective. They are also the sorts of shields that students tell me they use all the time and wonder why they don't feel any protection from the energies of the world around them. But my visualization was strong, and my mind's eye could see scraps of other people's feelings caught in the barbs of the fencing, and likewise held back by the solid wooden planks or welded wire of the wide fence below it. As these fences kept cows in the pasture and hens in the henyard, the visualization helped me get my arms around the notion of self-shielding at a time when it was imperative to do so. To this day, I will sit myself in the midst of that pasture and feel at home in the place my imagination and magic have built to protect me. It works every time, especially if my image includes a cuppa tea and a few oatmeal raisin cookies.

How Shields Work

On the whole, shields must be energetic boundaries that feel solid and impenetrable. They must be erected swiftly, and, because of that, you must find a technique that works for you and practice it until it is reliable. Shields often need to be erected when you are not at your best—another reason to be so adept in their raising that nothing can stop you doing that. I am a fan of science fiction and liken this to those great spaceships of our imagined future, the ones that have weaponry, strong shields, and science labs. In the teeth of an attack from the unknown, the captain of the ship will say to a crewmember, "Shields up." A handle is slid, a button is pushed, or a touchscreen is activated. Shields up.

From within your shields, you have a moment, like the crew of the starship, in which you can determine your next action. But you will not have that safety until you can quickly raise effective shields. Shielding is an act of self-care and I expect you to care enough for yourself to do it well. Too many of us are psychically on call all the time, at the beck and call of anyone who needs our time, our skills, or simply our attention. Some of you have shared your shielding techniques and have discovered that the way you raise and set your shields leaves gaps in your protection—and you are doing that on purpose so you can keep the connection with those who need you. Instead of making a safe battlement from which you can strategize and figure out what's knocked you off-balance, you are trying to protect yourself while wearing the sort of net bag that holds lemons at the grocery store.

Let's visualize for a moment. It is the middle of the day and you are doing exactly what you should be doing—working, creating, tending. Suddenly you feel strangely distracted and low energy. You slow what you're doing and ground yourself. Is it a physical illness of some kind? After years of pandemic survival, we really don't know what the next symptom might be, do we? From this place of confusion and need, and firm in your grounding (your soul and body in alignment and harmony), you raise your strong shields. They protect you on all sides as well as above your head and below your feet. Now you take a deep breath. No energy comes in and none goes out. You now have space in which to determine your next move. Is this something coming toward me or something I'm manufacturing? Those fast-as-lightning shields have given you a precious moment to breathe and think. If it is from within, bring yourself to a quiet place through your controlled breathing. If it is coming from outside, you have two choices—you can keep your shields up until the source has shifted or you can push back. Whichever one you choose, you are in the right place to put it in action.

Keeping Your Shields Up

If you are keeping your shields up for the time being, find something stable in your immediate vicinity that you can plug your shields into: the big tree in your yard, the engine of the car, your altar. Most things contain enough life force to charge your shields for an hour or so, so you can go on with your life. You plug into these things by establishing an energetic connection through touch, ideally. If this is not possible, you can use an adaptation of the Silver Thread method found in chapter 10: ground yourself and imagine a pulse of energy moving from your center, traveling along your body until it reaches the ground. Send the pulse to the ally you are requesting and let it rest on the object. Use your discernment to test whether your action is acceptable. Whatever ally you choose, it is appropriate to ask the thing if it will help you out.

Listen and if you feel the answer is no, move to the next thing. It will only take a moment and you will have practiced witchly good manners.

Pushing Back

Sometimes the intrusive energy creates a desire to push it away and not simply deflect it. If you choose to push back, you may do that in several ways. One method that is popular with my crowd is to imagine the outside of your shields turning to mirrors and the energy returning to the place it came from. No malice, no big deal. You don't need to waste time trying to decide the specifics of this intrusion: you merely allow it to bounce off and return to its place of origin. Your shields are tied to an energy source near you, and you go on with your day. Periodically you check your shields to make sure they are still strong, and you will spend a moment feeling the energy structure you have created to see if it is still needed.

A more advanced technique—which you will certainly be ready for in no time at all—is to tie your shields to the energy that they were raised to deflect. The more deeply engaged and stronger that energy is, the stronger your shields are. And when the source is redirected or ceases, your shields will feel saggy, and you can release them intentionally. It's a bit Marvel Comics, I know, but it is terribly helpful.

More focused pushback on these interferences requires slightly different techniques. which we will discuss at the end of this chapter when we look at banework.

Ways You Can Create Protective Shields

After graduating from the cattle fence shielding method, I finally came up with a method that comes easily to me and is effective no matter where I am or what mood I'm in. I will review for you the way I have found best. You can try this and see if it works for you. You may need to adapt it, of course, but the important thing is that you have a workable and protecting shield.

I do it quite quickly with a swirling gesture in my strong hand—and sometimes with both hands at once. But the steps are a little more elaborate. I ground and pull up a curved wall from the earth directly in front of me. It is taller than me but transparent. I pull the next one up on my right and the third one is behind me. The last wall is on my left and the entire structure melds together at each joint. Nothing comes in, nothing goes out. With a sweeping gesture of the same hand, I articulate a bowl-shaped curve that creates the same boundary under my feet. The last gesture sees my hand, fingertips pointed upward, move from my left to my right above my head in an arc. This stretches a dome above my head, a dome that completes the ball.

This dome can be made of any material, as long as you know it is strong and impermeable. Choose something that makes you feel loved, cozy, and safe. The bright quilt your grandmother made for you? Yes. Your partner's big sweater? Yes. Fat green cabbage leaves all around you and you sitting in the middle of a cabbage? Yes.

Most of my magics are based in the use of energy, but there are many other ways to feel protected and safe, to give you that brief moment in which to discern what is going on. There are talismans that one can wear, around neck or wrist or always kept in pocket, that are activated through touch. I tap my necklace and shields come up—that sort of thing.

Plants That Protect You

There are protective herbs that can be grown in your garden, worn as a circlet or jewelry, or distilled into oils to be pressed onto our skin or around the doorframe of your house to add protection. There is a long tradition of planting particular plants to repel enemies, spirits, or ill will. As with any substance that is ingested, breathed, or applied, take good care that it will not trigger an allergic reaction.

Some of my favorite protective plants include holly (*Ilex aquifolium*), rosemary (*Salvia rosmarinus*), hawthorn (*Crataegus monogyna*), mountain ash (*Sorbus americana*), stinging nettle (*Urtica dioica*), bloodroot (*Sanguinaria canadensis*), witch hazel (*Hamamelis virginiana*), ground cedar (*Diphasiastrum digitatum*), mugwort (*Artemisia vulgaris*), honey locust (*Gleditsia triacanthos*), and rue (*Ruta graveolens*). I always encourage you to use plants in your region, especially plants that are plentiful.

For me, native plants are the way to go. Simple and abundant plants like plantain, clover, and cleavers. Walk through your world and abide with the native plants you seem to see everywhere. Find their names and their habits. Not just finding their "uses," for they are not here only for humans to make use of their properties. Try to have a little respect. Some plants clean toxins from the soil, some add necessary minerals. We are only now acknowledging communication among plants, though there are cultures throughout the world that have known this since ancient times. If you are not familiar with the work on the mycelium road, there is plenty of new research on that and the concept of the Mother Tree. Science matching myth is a powerful mating.

Wards and Warding

All of this leads us to the shielding technique we call wards, or warding. This is the act of setting boundaries that lie beyond your personal field. These are ways to protect your house or your property, even your car. Strong wards around your house and property can lessen the need for personal shielding too, giving the place where you reside—where you eat and sleep—a boundary that catches much of the wandering energy that you may want to keep at bay.

All the reasons we outlined about personal shielding hold with setting wards, but the technique is a little different. I'll outline what I do—the steps and then the energetic shortcut—and we'll look at other ways to set these boundaries. Step one is clearing.

Clearing

As a village witch, I sometimes get called to clear the energy in a house or apartment, but the residents usually don't think of the outside, which may be where the problem lies. Here's a quick example of what I mean. The first thing I do is greet the resident and reassure them about the procedure. Then I walk through the building and note where there are temperature changes, odd bits of architecture, and household items that feel a little too lively. These can be thrift store finds or inherited treasures, and they have come into the house with a signature of their history attached to them.

Then I go outside, which often puzzles the person who called me. My little black bag always contains candy and liqueur for the spirits of the land, and I dig a little hole for a handful of bright candies and a splash of activating alcohol. Then I stand for a few minutes to feel my way to communication with the land and its spirits.

Silently, I explain what I'm up to and I ask for their help and for their noninterference, for they are curious and can be possessive. I make sure I am not shielded so they can feel my energy signature and understand I am not a threat.

It is only then, after observing this old-fashioned etiquette, that I return to the structure to do the work. Please note that I do not set wards before the work on the inside is finished. It is counter-productive to set up a boundary that I will want to traverse when I shift the energy around in the house. Following the clearing, I go back outside (usually on my way to my car) and set wards around house and then around the property.

Setting the Wards

Here is how I set the wards. As you practice this work, you will find the technique that works best for you.

I use a physical reminder, a talisman, that is the anchor for the energy field of the wards. Some of the things I use are glass beads (the sort that florists use in the bottom of arrangements) that are readily available wherever you find craft supplies and small pieces of gravel. If you live and work near the sea, you may choose small shells or sea glass. The talisman anchor you choose should not be something ephemeral or edible, though a small ball of aluminum foil can work in a pinch.

My preference is to set these anchors in the corners of the house, inside. Depending on the nature of the occupant and the building itself, this may not be possible. Toddlers and curious dogs may eat the anchors, which is bad, or will at the very least disrupt them. If the household has a fair amount of chaos, set the wards outside at the corners of the building. Usually doable with a house or duplex, but apartment buildings and dorms require a different technique. Bring a piece of soft chalk with you when you set up your kid in the dorm and use the chalk to draw a dot in each corner and on either side of the door. This functions as the anchor and stays in place surprisingly well. This works for your bedroom too if you live in a house or apartment with others or want to add an extra layer of protection for the place where you sleep.

After the building is warded, step to the literal boundaries of the property, if possible, and set anchors at the corners there. Many lots have been laid out in tidy rectangles, which makes this easy. But older lots or the yards of gardeners may be more challenging. If you can, wear tough clothing and sturdy shoes and get into the corners of the property, leaving a small chunk of gravel, a crystal, or a florist glass bead. If the resident has no idea where the boundaries are located, then set the wards in the accessible edges of the yard.

Attaching to Energy Source

Once the anchors are placed, attach them to an energy source in the landscape. You are getting good at sensing the liveliness of things around you, so take the time to figure it out. Large healthy trees are good. Big stones in the hardscaping work too. The lake at the end of the yard is a possibility too. An electric pole may work—they aren't often replaced. The point is that you are tying the wards into a source that will activate and energize them so neither you nor the resident have to do that. Wards set in this way have a good chance of offering protection that is reliable but not burdensome. A small pocket talisman or piece of empowered jewelry can also be a material reminder of your protection in the world.

Know Your Limits

This brings me to ley lines ... and a story. A ley line, if you are unfamiliar with the concept, is a strip of energy that flows on the surface of the earth. Ley lines often connect areas of significant cultural importance and can be studied through the exploration of geomancy.

I was called in to clear the energy in an old house in an old neighborhood. The occupant was someone I had known for years and knew to be of a nervous nature, shall we say. I came to the property with the expectation that it would be a straightforward job of work that would freshen up the energy in her house and relieve her of any anxiety about invisible residents.

It was one of the most complicated jobs I have ever done, down to the present day.

The house was crisscrossed with cold corridors and at the end of the visit, we determined that the previous ... and dead ... inhabitants were still in the attic. (I was working with a friend in those days, something I highly recommend.) The ladies were sisters and were not in any way malicious or harmful, but they were reluctant to leave. We bargained and begged, and it was finally determined that they would remain in the attic and would not be disruptive in the rest of the house. Unless someone came into the attic to get something stored there. Then they expected attention and probably a gift of some kind. This worked for the resident who only stored Christmas decorations there. She agreed that she would wrap a little box in her prettiest paper and leave it there for the ladies. (She did that for as long as she lived in the house.)

We dusted off our hands, fed the land spirits an especially large splash of coffee-flavored liqueur, and counted ourselves lucky. The resident contacted me two days later to say they were back and hanging out in her bedroom. This is not unusual, especially when the resident is amenable to the spirit folk remaining, proving that setting boundaries can be tricky no matter who they involve.

I scheduled a return visit. That's when I encountered the ley line.

Ley lines are stretches of earth energy that emerge onto the surface and are observable visually and through feel. I discovered them through wandering the byways of Britain and Ireland, where they seem to crisscross the landscape, often traveling between old sites that we now consider sacred in some way. When I returned to the southern highlands of Appalachia, I realized those fuzzy lines I'd been seeing my whole life were ley lines. For me, they were a part of the collection of things I see, like auras. I immersed myself in Alfred Watkins's book *The Old Straight Track*.[2]

This client was a terrible procrastinator. She had moved into this charming older house many years before but still had piles of boxes that had not been unpacked or tucked away. Her bedroom was full of these boxes as well as portable clothing racks because she had plans for the closets that hadn't been realized yet. The bed was lovely and obviously her refuge from a life that had grown too complicated to contain. A big stack of books covered both bedside tables, and she was proud of her voracious reading habits.

I am not sure how we missed that ley in the original visit. It is possible that the spirit ladies in the attic had grabbed our attention and we weren't thorough enough on the ground floor. It's also possible that the spirit ladies had kept the line repressed and had used it as their own energy source. In either case, here it was, big as life. I stepped into it, like stepping into a swift, cold stream. Not at all

---

2. Alfred Watkins, *The Old Straight Track: Its Mounds, Beacons, Moats, Sites, and Mark Stones* (Glastonbury, UK: The Lost Library, 2013).

unpleasant but not something you'd want shooting past the place that you sleep. Confident I'd found the source of the problem; I sat down with the resident and told her what I'd found.

She was fascinated and agreed that she didn't feel threatened by it: it was only an active presence that disturbed her rest. She asked if I could remove it or refocus it and I told her that was unlikely. I suggested she move her bedroom to one of the other rooms—the ones that held all those ragged stacks of unopened boxes. Oh, no, she couldn't do that. We could get you some help in rearranging things, I offered. No. Not possible. I would "have to" stop the ley line. I told her that wasn't possible, and she'd have to find someone else. I even suggested moving the bed or that she get out of bed on the opposite side, so she wasn't stepping into that lively stream. None of that was possible for her, so I left her there with the spirit ladies, the ley line, and her sad sickness.

She moved out several months later, then moved back in a year later. The last straw for her was finding mold behind some of the boxes—which had apparently moved with her and then moved back, still unpacked—and found a new place where she seemed to stick. I'd love to know who lives in that house now and what they've done with that room.

This story serves to illustrate a few things. Once you claim this work as your own, you will be asked by friends, then friends of friends, then strangers to fix the things in their lives that they can't understand. They will be broken people who need help and attention and solace. You can supply some of that.

It is also important to acknowledge the things you can't do. Too many people claim abilities they don't have—don't be one of them. Until you have mastered a thing, you can tell the seeker that you are learning and will give the problem a go but with no guarantees of success because you are new to this technique. You will learn best by trying things, but try not to allow unreasonable expectations to color your relationship with a friend or client.

There will be things you will never master and that is also okay. There will also be times when the protocol you have always trusted fails you. That is the nature of the work and of the earth changes that are happening in this time of global climate rearrangement.

Banework

Banework is a controversial subject in many communities, but folk magicians globally have engaged with this work, largely without any qualms. I often teach about the efficacy of banework and have frequently written about it, so this information will be merely an introduction and an explanation of the importance of engaging this work, if you are called to it.

If you are uncomfortable with the idea of this determined pushback, there is nothing that compels you to do this—nothing at all. We often speak of being "called" to do specific kinds of work, like being a death midwife or weather worker, and there's an implication that this calling is an indication that we are called to specific work because we have a stronger skillset in that area. Banework is no different. Those who are called to it will find themselves researching traditional practices and devising effective ways for returning energy to the place from which it came.

Banework is the word I choose for this work. I don't use black magic for a variety of reasons. To equate something that is considered dangerous and inappropriate even within parts of our own communities—not to mention the dominant culture without—with the word black is probably racist and is a way to further alienate cultures. The implication that black is evil and white is good plays on some very old tropes that hinder our desires to make the world a more egalitarian place. *Left-hand path* is another way to talk about this work (which I find insulting to left-handed people, who have long been vilified and condemned in Western culture for something over which they have no real control).

I've developed a list of the Nine Levels of Bane. It is divided into two sections. The first part is called "nonengagement" and doesn't require the magic-worker to do anything except general self-defense work. The second part is more direct action and is called "engagement." I developed the list when I began teaching my philosophy of banework, which I consider an advanced healing practice. Here it is, from the mildest to the strongest.

Levels of Bane: Nonengagement

The banes listed in the first half of the list aren't considered banework by most people. By beginning with these simple magics, many practitioners understand that this work doesn't have to include hot-tempered revenge. Throughout this list, the most effective working method is one of thoughtful and thorough consideration of how a situation or person can be healed by your actions.

1. Ignore the problem and hope it goes away.
2. Send good energy by lighting a candle or saying a prayer.
3. Set an energy trap or filter.
4. Set shields, then clear the energy inside your shields. Set wards.

Levels of Bane: Engagement

The second half of this list requires engagement. You may choose to give a warning by contacting the people involved, either verbally or energetically, but it isn't necessary to allow for a last chance before you act, especially before 8 and 9.

5. Reversal. Reversal returns the energy to the person or persons who sent it, whom we will refer to as the subject. You can do this several ways, including by placing a mirror near your front door or your home altar or by placing mirrored shields and wards around you and your property. You can create a doll (naming it The Person Who Is Messing with Me) and place it in the freezer or in a jar of vinegar.

6. Binding. If you know who the subject is, you have some advantages in your banework. Binding is a particularly useful tool to stop harassment in its tracks. You can bind your subject through a wrapped egg that bears the subject's name and misdeeds, and then place the egg in the freezer. You can use a photograph in the same way.

7. Destruction of resources and/or support, facilitating a shift of luck. Sometimes the best way to facilitate healing in a situation is to remove the powerbase of your subject. If the subject is employing a glamour, you can dissolve it in the way we discuss in chapter 10.

8. Banishing, shunning, or separation from community. You can remove the subject from your life, using all available techniques. The subject can be ghosted and ignored. As you remove your energy from the subject, you will find that they are mentioned in your presence less and less frequently. A technique I have employed for this is to write the subject's name on a piece of paper and drop it in the toilet to be flushed away from my house and my life. It is vitally important to stop talking

about the subject to mutual friends and to refrain from gossiping, which continues to link your energy. Let the subject go completely.

9. Finishing bane. This is the most controversial of banes and should only be taught teacher to student and only employed after the deepest consideration. In all my years of practice, I have never gotten to this place, and I suspect you won't either. There are so many other choices, and I encourage you to try those.

These suggestions are merely that, and they are the ones I use when doing banework. If you choose this work, you will find other techniques and will evaluate their effectiveness. Remember, you need never do any of this. Ever. Your magical practice will be no less useful if you step back from banework. You are not more powerful or more of a witch for doing this work. If it calls you, try it. If it disturbs you, let it be.

Feeling Attacked?

Most of us are not under a regular and concerted energetic attack and that is the truth of it. There is no doubt that there are people you will meet who have a knack for pulling energy from other people. They are often attracted to people who are high-energy achievers. Their numbers are not large, however, and when you learn to identify them, you can easily disrupt them. We'll look at that in chapter 10.

Most of us have that one friend who seems to always be under near-constant "psychic attack." If they are having an off day, someone yells at them, or they are feeling guilty about something they feel they should have done but haven't, they will assume someone has attacked them. Two things to remember—most people aren't thinking about you at all, much less directing targeted venom at you to bring you down. Also, the vast majority of people simply don't have the skillset to do such a thing. Someone may be righteously angry with you and wish you ill, but they don't have the first idea about how to do that. In my world of folk magic, I am often approached by people who are convinced that someone has "thrown a root" or "rooted" them, and it's the same thing. Life is not going well; circumstances are not running in their favor, and it can't be their fault. It must indicate that someone means them harm and is targeting them.

This does happen, to be fair. There are some people who are perfectly capable of wreaking havoc through their malice or of hiring someone to do the work for them. But the first thing to consider may be your personal practice and the general state of your life. You might choose to check the astrological events, the phase of the moon, and whether (or not) you have been doing your self-care. You may be emotionally and energetically depleted because of your workload or schedule. Look at your life and see if these troublesome things that seem to be happening are as big or dangerous as you think at first. Go to your altar if you are a theist. Take stock of your life and immediate surroundings, and you will often find that your plate is too full, you are spinning too many plates, and your best practice is to learn to set boundaries and to say no.

◈

NOW YOU TRY

Being confident about shielding in all its forms is helpful in our chaotic and challenging world. This chapter gave us some techniques but stressed the importance of having a protocol that works well and quickly.

Do you have a protective technique that always works for you? Do you switch between effective techniques, finding the one that fits the situation and your mood? Is there a shielding technique here that appeals to you? Practice it several times a day for three days and make a note of how often and how well it worked.

Hint: Shielding can be done anywhere but should be done as swiftly as possible. Shields up! Aye, Captain!

Chapter 9
Living as a Witch

This book happily encourages all who read it to fall in love with magic and do it all the time, happily and successfully. But that invitation flies in the face of most of human history, throughout which the people who have harnessed the life vitality that we call energy have been deemed dangerous and evil. It isn't only Western culture. In much of the world's folklore, those who carry the keys to these dark kingdoms are held in contempt and viewed with fear, with loathing.

Even in our present day, there are places in the world where an accusation of practicing witchcraft, of being a witch, is an excuse to torture and murder the odd, the old, the suspicious. This chapter is about perils and pitfalls of being a witch and how to work around them and be inspired by those magical workers of the past. It is also about setting personal intentions: the intention we set for a particular working and the overall intention we set for our lives as magic-workers.

Examining Your Intentions

Throughout this book, I have reviewed many of the stepping stones of a solid magical practice, including several ways to ground, to shield ourselves, to draw and to harvest workable energy into our battery, and to send that energy where we will. I often recommend that students also consider a catchall intention for the purpose of practice. Make it something simple to remember and, if possible, measurable, giving yourself a way to check your effectiveness. When you do a parking spell, for instance, you know it works if you find a place to park your car. When practicing, it isn't so important to see an immediate result. You can choose something more general—like finding humane solutions for homelessness. You can monitor statistics to see if the number of homeless people in your city changes and make a mental note of it. But the importance of setting the focus is to help you practice sending energy.

When forming an ethical magical practice, it is vitally important to weave a clear and precise intention for what we will and won't do as part of that practice. One of the best parts of being a witch and a Pagan is that your personal ethics are not monitored by nor imposed by a central authority. Each of us works our way through the world according to our own lights. You are not forced by a religious authority to conform to ethics incompatible with your moral compass.

When you are creating an intention for your work, you will necessarily be informed by your system of ethics and your moral compass as well as your personal history. Don't rush into a statement of intention because you feel outraged or sorrowful. You may even choose to write down all the possibilities and cross out the ones that feel too large or too vague. A single strong and achievable action statement will serve you well. For one thing, you will be able to discern whether the working is effective. For another, you will have a clear image of the desired outcome. Vagary and caprice will not serve you well as you set intentions.

"My intention is to put an end to all war" is a noble sentiment but is too broad to be accomplished and too vague to be monitored effectively. "My intention in this working is to shield the people of that village from as much destruction as possible" is more manageable.

Your Choice, Your Way

As with the basic techniques for magical practice, you get to search your ethics and conscience and decide what's best for you. There is no licensing agency and no bureaucracy to slow you down or reject you. Witches have always stood outside law but within culture, which has not afforded us much safety or respect, but for a while there was a nice supply of chickens.

There are people who will tell you there are many parts of practicing magic that should be avoided at all costs. It isn't just the banework that we discussed in the previous chapter. These warnings include the casual use of cultural traditions other than your own and interfering with others' free will.

Identifying a Personal Ethical System

Unless you belong to one of the spiritual systems that proscribe its adherents' actions, the questions involving your personal ethics are questions for you alone. The majority of any group seems to agree on some things while agreeing to disagree on others. When affinity groups bump into each other, the issues can become more complicated. Reasonable heads can often find ways to consensus, but not all heads are reasonable. For the sake of your work here, it is sufficient that you examine your personal history and creed and go with the information they supply you. In any case, if you feel uneasy in any energetic work, it is vital that you understand the source of the discomfort. It is only from this place that you can decide what is best for your practice and for you.

Cultural Appropriation

Cultural appropriation is an issue writ large in the Pagan and Pagan-affiliated spiritual communities, with pros and cons on every position. In my Appalachian writing, I refer to this as "cultural strip-mining"—the act of removing valuable and desirable pieces of a particular culture while having little respect and even contempt for the original practitioners and returning nothing to the culture that is left depleted by our actions.

Approaching spiritual technologies that are not native to you is a matter for serious consideration. It is also a question for your personal ethics. Learning from a practitioner steeped in the ways of their own culture and then practicing with the permission of that teacher and the implied permission of the cultural group may be completely different from learning from someone who is not from a specific culture and learning the technology from a source not imbedded in the culture. But you may choose to observe such teachings with curiosity and never practice them personally. Educating ourselves on the cultures that are adjacent to our own helps us better understand people and groups that are not our own, easing the way to better communication as well as cooperation.

Free Will

The other debate has to do with interfering with the free will of another person, and many people are unwilling to do so. In an effort to make the world a more equitable and just place, interfering with the actions of the people who are making the world worse has to be part of the tool kit for workings. If you can't decide on better or worse at the moment—a religious and political knife edge that some of us have set ourselves upon—it may make sense not to interfere and to leave well enough alone. Shakespeare's Hamlet says it best: "rather bear those ills we have / than fly to others we know not of."[3] There are times and situations that do require direct intervention, and it will be up to you to examine your heart and conscience to decide what you will do as well as what you will not do.

A Shifting Community of Witches

Along with any cultural baggage, modern witches often must face the legacy of modern Pagan spiritual practice as it changes and, we hope, evolves. When Wicca was being formulated and codified, there was an emphasis on how nonthreatening modern Witches are. The word *witch* was used by Wiccans to denote a Wiccan practitioner, but because that word is loaded with folkloric chains, it was important to also stress that Wiccans "harm none," a tenet of Wicca, and that Wicca is a modern adaptation of much older fertility religions. That's why you will read about people who practice "white" magic, not "black" magic. In many of these traditions, for example, cursing and hexing are not allowed, and there is a strong insistence that baneful magic is never a part of approved practice.

Decades later, we began reading about "gray" magic and "green" magic, the latter being focused on the flora of the natural world. People began to describe themselves as hedge witches or traditional

---

3. William Shakespeare, *The Tragedy of Hamlet, Prince of Denmark, Folger Shakespeare Library Edition* (New York: Simon and Schuster, 1992), act 3, scene 1, lines 89–90.

witches to denote someone who practices witchcraft but is not Wiccan. It has taken us several generations since the founding of Wicca to get to the place where we can separate the craft of magic from the practice of a religion or spirituality whose adherents call themselves witches and call what they do the Craft or the Old Craft.

Working for Others

Once you've gotten the hang of this work, you may be asked by others to do it for them. Many people are looking for answers and for help, and people like us sometimes have the answer they need. Please don't take on this work for others until you're good at it. That seems logical, but I am often shocked at the level of incompetence that permeates the fields of magic work, including divination. Don't pretend to be something you aren't to achieve status or notoriety. You will only hurt or embarrass yourself and turn people off with your inadequacy. Learn your stuff, then share, if asked.

There is one more point I want to make here, a comment on something I have seen too many times to ignore. Some people achieve a certain status and no little fame from their insistence on their sensitivity. They claim the title of *empath* because it affords them a special place in our Pagan communities and cultures. The work of an empath is not merely to feel the people and events around them. The responsibility that goes with that work bears consideration. When we discussed auric fields and halos, we understood that seeing such things may encourage you to speak with the person who is being held in them. We must tread carefully from there: deciding the how and where and if of disclosing the information that you see to the person it directly affects. We ask ourselves if we're absolutely sure of what we see and how that information may best be disclosed.

In my opinion, if you claim the role of an empath, you are also taking on this obligation. Your ability to feel the inner emotional workings of another person is not a parlor trick so that you can show off in front of the assembled group. It is a continuous job of work where you walk through the world as a servant to your craft and you do your best to alleviate suffering. When we use words like *empath* or describe ourselves as "highly sensitive," it isn't an excuse to sit in the corner with a cool towel on your forehead and be tended by people with better things to do. Don't be seduced by the status of the words you have chosen to describe yourself.

If the input is truly too much for you and you are not using it as a status marker in your group, the practice of effective shielding is a necessity. You are not cutting yourself off from this input forever—you are giving yourself a break from it. Instead of a cool cloth and a bevy of handmaidens, try getting your shields up and taking a break by walking in nature, drinking some water, taking a nap. When we talk of self-care, this is also a part of that. We do no good for our community, our family, or ourselves when we refuse to do adequate shielding. We are instead being self-indulgent and attention-seeking. Is that really what our work is? No, I don't think so either.

Charging for Work

When you are in that good place, you have another decision to make: whether or not to charge for your work. Let's consider that for a moment.

For years, we have argued about whether magic-workers should charge for the work we do. There are powerful arguments on both sides—if you don't charge for your services, there is a strong possibility that the work will not be valued in our capitalist culture and your advice will be ignored. On the other hand, charging money as opposed to bartering or "exchanging energy" can put you in the same place as the contractor who fixes your bathroom wall. There are expectations that money results in an equal value in services rendered. If the esoteric issue isn't resolved to the satisfaction of the client who is now more of a customer, you may have to deal with resolving additional problems. Some people believe that you will lose your ability to do the work if you charge for a magical gift you were given.

The decision—as with most things magical—must be up to the individual witch. An example that is often invoked is the summoning up of a bucolic fantasy witch world. Work is bartered for; chickens and eggs are often mentioned. Folklore and Hollywood tell us that witches must be offered booze, smokes, and sex, as though the whole of witchcraft is set in California's 1940s noir style. None of those chickens or other food items will pay your rent or utilities, in case you hadn't noticed. The place where you fill up your car with gas will take cash or card, hardly ever chickens.

As traditional as our practices may be, we live in the twenty-first century and not all things in life can be bartered for, so we must needs have recompense in some way. You may also choose what you charge for and to whom you charge it.

Some clients are in a place where an outlay of cash is a challenge, and we must decide if we are going to charge cash money or let it slide. In every circumstance where I have been discerning and compassionate about a client's predicament, it has always ended well. The client either returns when they have some money, sends some money that I wasn't expecting, or refers me to someone who is generous. It always seems to work out and I don't remember ever regretting generosity.

Since there are no hard-and-fast rules, you can choose to charge for some services but not others. I almost always charge for tarot readings, which gives me the flexibility to give some away when the need arises. I charge for energy clearings and the amount depends on how far I have to travel and how long it will take. You can certainly create a sliding scale for any charges and also offer a "friends and family" rate. I don't do much work for hire, but I do create spellwork and meditations for people who seem to have much need and little knowledge. I don't charge for that.

Like many of you, I am also a priestess and am ordained clergy, licensed in several states. I always charge for weddings and hand-fastings, and—as with house and other energy clearings—the rate depends on distance traveled as well as the amount of time it takes. Use your best intuition and honor your time and your worth. I had a friend who only accepted gift cards to the local grocery chain as payment, but I take cash, check, or PayPal.

I never charge for funerals, memorials, or for blessing the body of the deceased, though people will often slip me an envelope that contains a thank-you card and some money. I really enjoy rituals that are specific to the needs of the family and the desires of the person whose life is the focus of the ceremony. Adding your loving connection to the earth and your adept energy work will create a memorial that allows for the grief cycle to commence for the family and friends of the beloved.

Obviously, it is best not to charge for services if you are new to the work or not effective yet in your practice of it. Let your intuition be your best guide about these things and try not to compare yourself to others who may be charging more because they have more experience and a strong success rate. Or because they are full of themselves and assume they are worth as much as their mama tells them they are.

You can check with other people in your area and see what the going rate is for the things you're asked to do. Use that as a general guide. This isn't two rival grocery stores having a price war about half-gallon jugs of milk. You only need a vague idea—a ballpark figure—to give you a range of possible charges.

You can save yourself all of that and simply not charge anything, but I hasten to remind you that your time, ability, and knowledge are valuable, and people tend to have more respect for things that are paid for. Bartering is another way of paying for services rendered, but it will be up to you to determine what a fair trade is.

I had a tarot client who had never had a reading from me before. She proudly presented me with ten two-dollar bills and a couple of empty canning jars because she knew I could use them. Her hour-long consultation was quite a bargain compared to my usual rate— but I did get those two jars.

Working Alone and with Others

Covens are a traditional—and perhaps stereotypical—organizing unit for magic-workers. You will encounter covens of all sizes and compositions: women only, men only, numbering from four (enough to call the Quarters) to infinity, or as many as your gathering space will hold. Some Western magical traditions declare a specific number but, for the most part, covens are the size of the number of people who have the time and inclination to meet and work together.

Much of this book is aimed at those who choose to practice alone, and things are different if you choose to do this work in a group, including the energetic dynamics and the interplay of personal power. It can feel like seventh grade all over again, and if that happens, please consider a quiet and firm exit. But it can be quite gratifying and certainly educational.

I was part of a largish coven for many years. We met most Saturday evenings, and we watched babies arrive, children grow into teenagers, and teens reach for adulthood. Marriages dissolved too, and that was one reason we ultimately stopped meeting. My daughter's First Blood ritual was one of the last we did as a group— and that was only the women. The covenstead is now the little farm I write about in *Seasons of a Magical Life*. We worked through a consensus model to set our intention for any work, and that engagement gave us a corporate strength that our individual selves couldn't achieve. That is one of the best reasons to cultivate a working relationship with others—we can combine energies to achieve the desired intention, and our power is more than the sum of our parts.

Coven and circle work is not for everyone. Too many people have come through that experience with deep trauma and are leery to return to it, just as many are leery to return to the toxic religions of their childhood. But if you and a few friends are interested in creating a magical circle, I encourage you to try—and to keep your eyes open.

Dealing with Fear: Yours and Others'

Many of us carry a powerful fear of this work, as well as a general fear of success. Fear can be a terrible deterrent to living the life we desire, a stumbling block to authenticity. Working through our fears, which generally grow from our personal experience with authority and punishment, is a separate path, and I encourage you to take that road as you can. If your fears are ingrained and difficult to budge, please remember that none of these exercises is required. Go slowly and feel your way: take your time and challenge the fears you can, so they can begin to serve you. Or find the ways to live with them by acknowledging their origins and working around them.

We are so easily bullied and influenced in these days of massive information coming to us through our phones and monitors, through social media and social interactions. Determining in a gentle but thorough way what is important work for you—what I call your "heart work"—is a vital step in claiming the practice of magic.

These comforting tropes about how "safe" modern witches are serve several purposes:

Keeps Us Safe from the Crazies

As long as the general public continues to believe that witches and magic-workers are soft-headed and delusional but basically harmless, we are safer in a world where anything out of the societal norm is suspect and potentially dangerous. But being more mainstream—as witchery is now—is no real shield either. It is so easy to fall out of favor, both in the social media world and in your own neighborhood. Being an openly practicing witch is not and has never been a safe way of life. No matter how much we soften the image or sugarcoat the practice, the word itself is a trigger for many people. I don't say this to discourage you or make you fearful but to remind you of the world we inhabit. You can choose to be completely private in your practice or to wear the stereotypical "witch" clothes you want to the grocery store or anything in between. If this is the work you are called to do, you will find a way that works best for you and your family.

Makes the Religion Part of It
Seem More Like a "Real" Religion

In the United States, we have a notion that each citizen has the freedom to practice the religion of their choice and cannot be forced to follow either their neighbors' religion or a state-sponsored one. The reality is much more complex, of course, and nonbelievers often have some religious claptrap forced upon them through state-sponsored Christian holidays or through intimidation by their neighbors or other citizens. Sometimes these can be countered through the legal system, but that challenge usually comes at a steep emotional and financial price, one that many cannot pay, and so they keep their collective heads down and hope for the best.

Repudiates the Stereotype and Reminds
Others That We're Human

Years ago, a friend brought his little son to the bookstore where I worked. The boy was about four years old and had seen a billboard near his house that featured a green-faced, warty, pointy-hat-wearing witch. The image terrified the boy and his dad explained that the picture wasn't a real witch, only a Hallowe'en one. The boy wasn't hearing it and was retriggered every time they drove down that stretch of street, finally putting his stuffed toy over his face so he couldn't see the "mean witch." My friend brought him to the bookshop because the boy had known me from an early age and also knew I was a witch.

It was sad to see this tough little guy so scared, but he let me take his hand and we walked back to the jolly children's section and set up camp in the readers' gazebo. At first, I listened to his description of the mean witch, an image that loomed large in his imagination. Then he said—you're a witch. Yes, I am. I put out both hands and he gingerly touched them, looking for a sign that everything would be okay. He patted my palm with both of his small hands. I talked to him about picking herbs and petting cats, and he reminded me that his cat liked me and sat on my lap. Finally, he crawled out of the little space and went to the Hallowe'en display, where he gathered a pile of books. He brought them to me and we read the "scary witch" ones first, then he climbed into my lap for the rest of the stack.

He was lucky because he knew an actual witch, and his dad suspected that spending time in one of his favorite places with someone kind would help relieve his anxiety. But not everyone has a witch friend to visit, and this image looms large in our collective consciousness.

How Representation in Fiction Affects Modern Witches

In addition to this reasoning, the representation of witches and magic-workers can make us fearful of our practice and too eager to listen to the finger-waggers on social media and elsewhere who are only too happy to control what we do and how we think.

Gives us an excuse to divide the kinds of people doing this work into separate camps and then focus our ire on each other, practicing less and talking about it more. In my world, you can set all that aside, refrain from yet another argument on social media about what is and is not "allowed," and choose to practice techniques until you understand them and can do them well.

A Legacy of Fear

We are told to never trust these unearthly beings—for they are often believed to be something other than human. We are taught to fear them, to fear what they do. The acts of healing are welcome, but even those are suspect, for someone who can heal must have great power and it would be such a simple thing to turn that power to malice and vengeance.

Let's look at some of those stories and characters and then turn our thoughts to how this culturally imbedded folklore may affect our desire (and courage) to practice magic. In a culture that condemns so much of what witches do in our work to make the world better, we should consider what those stories show us about practicing witchcraft and how witches stand outside the dominant culture.

The deliciously creepy story by W. W. Jacobs called "The Monkey's Paw" is a cautionary tale about the uses of magic and how dangerous it can be to have wobbly intentions when it comes to wishes and intentions.[4] Stephen King's novel *Pet Sematary* echoes the warning about wishing the dead back to life.[5] And the wonderful old ballad *The Wife of Usher's Well* weaves the sorrowful magic of a mother grown mad with grief for her lost sons.[6] These are three examples of a literary history that warns the reader away from the uses of magic, even in the form of wishes.

Folklore and fairy tales from many cultures also warn us away from the magic-workers who might teach us. In the well-known story of "Hansel and Gretel," a blind witch lives in a candy-trimmed

---

4. William W. Jacobs, *The Monkey's Paw and Other Tales of Mystery* (Chicago: Academy Chicago Publishers, 1997).

5. Stephen King, *Pet Sematary* (New York: Gallery Books, 2002).

6. Francis James Child, ed., *The English and Scottish Popular Ballads* (New York: Houghton, Mifflin and Company, 1904), 168–70.

house in the woods. Two abandoned children are caught, the boy is fattened up for supper, and the girl saves them both. We never see the witch doing any magic, but we have been thoroughly warned that witches can't be trusted and are potential cannibals as well.

The story of "Rapunzel" features a witch who makes a bargain with her neighbor, a pregnant neighbor who is craving greens from the witch's walled garden. It is the usual over-the-top bargain, in which the witch trades a mess of greens for the child when it's grown. In the end, the witch either meets a dreadful end or, in some versions, she simply disappears from the story.

From stories like these, we understand that witches are clever and tricky, always dangerous. They are willing to take advantage of people and situations to gain their perverse desires. Few people hearing those tales would choose to be the ugly, child-eating witch. There is no discernable magic, whether for good or ill, only malignant characters to avoid.

Baba Yaga

Baba Yaga comes to us from the Slavic countries of eastern Europe, where she figures prominently in many tales. She is a wild woman, an old woman, who lives in the darkest of forests. Her house stands on chicken legs and can move about to take advantage of sunset and moonrise. She flies through the night in a large mortar and uses a pestle as the rudder for her homely ship. Her rickety fence is decorated with flaming skulls. What's not to love? She even shows up in a children's book by Patricia Polacco, *Babushka Baba Yaga*.

Baba means "grandmother" or "old woman," and *Yaga* is difficult to pinpoint. It may mean "dirty" or "horrible." This gives you an idea that is familiar to anyone who has studied the concept of witches in early modern Europe. Old, repulsive woman who bears extraordinary powers. A dangerous and wild being that we must encounter in order to prosper or to grow. Her folklore warns women against wildness and the unauthorized use of power because those things—being our natural selves—can lead to exile and a lonely, meager life.

The best-known story of Baba Yaga involves the beautiful Vasilisa, a motherless child far from home, who carries a magical poppet that gives her motherly advice. She meets Baba Yaga and is given impossible tasks (which she accomplishes). When the chores are finished, Baba Yaga keeps her work and gives Vasilisa a human skull torch to take back to light up her house.

Here we see a witch who is formidable but who keeps her word. Vasilisa does not choose to stay with the fearful being (who at least behaves with honor) and goes back to the world she knows with the terrible people who inhabit it. The hearer of this tale understands that even if a witch appears to have a moral code, it is best to return to the ways you know, hard though they are.

Circe

Many female figures in folklore, as we've observed with these fairy tales, are relegated to supportive roles in a larger story, to dangerous but surmountable adversaries, or to weak victims who require rescue. Circe falls into that second category. Much of her lore comes down to us from Homer's *Odyssey*, where she is a demigod (a demigod is the child of a god and a mortal) and a sorceress. She lives on Aeaea, an island that lies on the route that Odysseus takes as he returns home from the Trojan War.

Circe has come to represent a wild woman who is tamed by a standard hero character, reminding those who hear her story that wild power must always be subdued by domestication. For women, the message has a Disney princess effect—the beautiful but unhappy woman is transformed by a man's "love." Domestication smooths all the rough edges and makes the wild (i.e., powerful) manageable, contained, and serviceable, thereby removing the danger.

Through this we understand that witches (who in traditional tales are almost always women) are broken, longing for love and family as defined by the dominant culture.

La Befana

Some witches fare better than others in the public mind, folklorically speaking. La Befana is a sweet Italian witch who has joined forces with the Church to celebrate Epiphany for children. In the Jesus story, three wise men (or kings or astrologers or magi) seek out the newborn, bringing expensive and symbolic gifts.[7] This is celebrated as Epiphany and occurs several days after the customary celebration of the natal event.

She is mostly harmless—we might think of her as "chaotic good"—as she flies from house to house, goes down chimneys and delivers her annual and benign judgment on behavior. The only danger from her presence is the lump of coal, which can be used for heat and food preparation, and her disheveled self often leaves soot on the hearth. She is an old and generous peasant woman, not at all wild (like Circe and Baba Yaga), tying her yearly pilgrimage to the popular Christian holy time.

We don't see La Befana in her natural state but as a cheerful servant of the Church. She bears all the exciting novelty characteristics of the folkloric witch—she is an old woman who flies around

---

7. Matthew 2:1–12 (KJV).

on a broom. She is often depicted in a headscarf and comfy shawl, as a round and doting grandmother.

How We Are Harmed

The lessons are clear to us, down to the current time: the untamed and powerful, even within ourselves, must be subdued, punished. Friendly and domestic is much preferred and in much less personal danger from the community at large. We internalize this, even now, when we limit our use of power to the soft and domestic arts. Those arts have great value, of course, no argument there. But they are not the only kind of workings that require our magic and our good attention.

These stories—and so many others—illustrate the dangers inherent in the scary old woman with special powers. Imagine how different the world's cultures would be if that solitary magic-worker was not a warning to behave in all the ways that society demands or else face the devastating magic of the witch. Imagine if she were a healer who held the secrets of the natural world, a beloved and important member of her community. A person who is helpful and clever—and maybe a little odd.

There may seem to be many different areas to consider as we develop a personal practice. We walk in a world where authenticity is highly valued but not easily discovered. Creating a helpful and personally enriching practice will require discernment as we wade through the morass of folktales and popular culture depictions of this creature we call a witch. Ethics, image, history, and practice are key elements of being a successful magic-worker. You can take those elements one at a time to avoid being overwhelmed. Except for the practice, which we should do as often as possible in order to be good at this esoteric work we have chosen for ourselves.

We live in a time now when claiming a witch aesthetic is very cool—smoky eyes, bone necklaces, collections of crystals and candles. Does that make them witches? Can you be a witch without practicing witchcraft, without doing magic? My answer is no. Absolutely not.

NOW YOU TRY

This chapter explores some of the old roots of our collective fears around making magic and learning through trial and error, which is the best way to learn this experiential craft. Many new witches are afraid to try things out because there is a deep fear that "doing it wrong" will have monumentally tragic results. We also looked at the difference between our intention as magic-workers and the specific intention that must be set for effective magical practice.

Who is your favorite folkloric or fairy tale witch and why? What are the properties that endear that character to you? Spend some time with your journal and see what you discover about your choice. You may find that she holds the key to some secrets you've held for many years.

Spend a moment every day—maybe while brushing your teeth—to remind yourself that you are a very lucky person. Do this for a week and see how you react to the unexpected during that time. Does your luck "hold"?

> *Hint: Pick out a lucky talisman to keep with you and attach some of your good luck to it. You can do that simply by holding it in your hand and saying, "What a lucky thing you are!"*

Chapter 10
Some Simple Workings

This final chapter includes some simple magics to make the day run more smoothly—parking, finding the items in the shop, shifting your mood, sending healing, healing yourself, and gathering resources to make your life work a little more smoothly.

This may be the chapter you've been waiting for, but I hope not. I debated with myself about whether to include anything about my personal workings in this book since the purpose of the thing is to encourage you to be creative in your workings and not simply copy someone else's stuff.

I want you to think of these examples as just that—templates for a way of doing these simple magics, a recipe that you are free to add on to or take away from to make a working that appeals to your tastes.

Several of my books have contained sample workings, and I have not included those here, for the most part. Where I have included them, the working has been reconstructed and retooled to reflect the way in which I do the work now. If you choose to compare notes, you can see how the methodology has changed, whether it is simpler or more complicated. I suspect, for the most part, the working has become more streamlined and efficient.

These are truly simple magics to make the day run more smoothly and help iron out the wrinkles and flatten some of life's bumps. A few take a longer view of life and its surroundings.

I want you to begin workings with something you actually need. Too often, we become so enamored of the uses of power that we get ourselves in a pickle by driving a sportscar when we can barely ride a tricycle. Take this step by step and try not to rush ahead of where you are. Having the firm base of knowing the steps makes getting behind the wheel of that sportscar exciting but not frightening. There is an old-fashioned statement: start as you mean to go on. Start with the basics you've been practicing and put them to work in the things you need, then move on from there.

Parking

I like to start with parking because I live in a city where parking can be very difficult. If you live in a place with good public transportation, you may not consider this an important skill. But for most of us, it can be a helpful thing to do well.

There are so many interesting ways to do this—ask your like-minded friends what kinds of rhymes and schemes they use to secure parking. You will meet Asphalta and Squat, goddesses of urban spaces. You will see examples of bribing particular spirits to be your guides in the endeavor. There are magic words for parking and chants to help visualize an empty space precisely where you need it. As you explore the possibilities, you will find the combination that works for you. And as you simplify your technique, you may end up doing something similar to this:

I rely on my will and solid intention-setting to do the job. After I fasten my seatbelt, I place both hands on the steering wheel, ground myself, and think, "I am going to the library (or wherever I am going) and I need a place to park." That's it. I may repeat the intention as I leave my neighborhood or as I sit at the first traffic light going out of my neighborhood, but often I do not.

Healing Bruises

This may seem trivial to you, but I have always bruised easily and dramatically. Spectacular blooms the color of spring irises arise at the least jarring poke. You can certainly choose to put a cotton pad soaked in witch hazel ointment on the area—an old herbal remedy that generally works.

But you can also try this, which I find works in most cases. As with all the work I do, I begin with deep grounding, a protocol that you should be more adept at by this point in your practice. Once I feel that satisfying energetic click that straightens my spine and shoulders, I place my strong hand over the affected area and circle it counterclockwise and palm down. I repeat either aloud or to myself, "Flow, my blood, flow around. Don't pool there under the skin but continue on your way. Flow, my blood, flow on through." By now you understand that the words are less important than the intention behind them, so say the words that help you connect with the mechanics of blood flow and with your physical self or say no words at all.

Healing Green Soaking Tub

A rough tumble or an impending cold may give you the desire for a little healing self-care. This also works if you're feeling low energy, anxious, or overly tired. I use the descriptor *green* here to suggest the natural healing energies we use for the working. You will be recharging your batteries with the energy that you've learned to gather from the world under your feet, the moon over your shoulder, and that barking dog next door. The visualization is the sweetest part of this working, so take your time and create the place you'd like to soak. My original vision was from my childhood—an old cattle trough made of concrete that sat on the mountain where I roamed freely. It was fed by a small spring and the water was always clean and cold. In my mind's eye, it became a spacious tub, almost big enough to swim in, where I could float under the sky, shaded by the old tree that partly covered it. In the visualization, the spring became a hot spring and the water took on a pleasant shade of green. There I floated and allowed the energy to salve my wounds, whether of body or spirit.

The most recent vision involves a wooden soaking tub but is otherwise unchanged. I sit on the perfect seat as the warm water rises up past my shoulders, almost to my chin. My body seems to float just above the seat as I bring the healing into my body.

Let me hasten to say that, if circumstances permit, an actual tub in which you can soak and access the extra healing energy is also a marvelous idea.

Drawing in Resources: Job, Time, Money

As a tarot reader, I know when my clients have generalized needs as well as more specific ones. I will tap a pentacles card and look directly at them. It is a good time for you to gather in your resources. The fact is we all need different resources at different times in our lives, sometimes all at once, but more often we need to target specific needs. Let's review some of the things you might need: money, time, friends, luck, and creativity.

Money is the resource we need to control so many aspects of life. It buys groceries, it pays the rent and utilities, it's good to have on hand if your friend needs help with a car repair. Credit is handy if you are looking to get a car or house or go to school after high school. Whether it's a credit card or a bank loan, gathering in credit or repairing your credit if it's weak can be important. Healing is self-explanatory and can include physical healing, emotional healing, and relational and community healing.

Many of us simply need more time to do the things we either need to do or want to do. We may need more people in our lives—friends or personal or professional networks. It is always handy to have good luck, but for many of us, we feel our luck has soured and needs a reboot. This can also happen with our creativity.

Determining the specific need can go far in making the working effective. A general "I need more!" will not serve you well, as you know from our discussion of intention.

Choosing from Several Things or Help in Making a Tricky Choice

Sometimes we are offered so many options that it becomes difficult to choose. This is true in so many areas. Here is one way to aid the decision-making process.

Place a wide-mouthed glass jar on a table in an area you are frequently in, like the kitchen table or your work area. Surround it with little slips of paper big enough to write on. Have a pen or pencil nearby. When you think of one of the options, write it down and put it in the jar. When the jar is full, wait a couple of days and remove a slip each time you are near the jar. Read what's on the paper and either keep it by laying it on the table by the jar or get rid of it in the recycling bin. Work your way through the jar until only the few bits of paper you chose are left. Lay those out in front of you on the table and let your hand rest on each in turn, then let your heart guide you in your choice.

Worries

Modern life has presented us a plethora of issues that we don't have a cultural way to address or repair without the use of therapy and medication. Those are two valuable choices that can be part of your sewing basket of healing possibilities for things like anxiety and lingering grief. You can also try a couple of simple spells to ease your burdens.

Set a pretty bowl on that same frequently used table and surround it with small rocks. When the bolt of anxiety or worry strikes you, pick up one of the stones and hold it in your hand, acknowledging the issue. Set your worry into the stone and place it in the bowl carefully, releasing the worry for now. You may choose to pick it up again, but people rarely do. When the bowl is full, place it under the moon—either outside or on a windowsill—and then take it away, leaving it in a driveway or parking lot with other plain stones. I keep one of these on my desk most of the time, and it is a simple repository for the things I choose not to carry.

You can also use a strong wind, like the ones that usher in a coming storm, to release those bolts of worry, anxiety, and grief. Speak your concern into the palms of your hands and stand with your back to the prevailing wind. Move your arms and hands out to either side of your body with your hands still palms up, and allow the wind to blow that concern away from you.

Travel

As most of you know, I love to travel and do so with gusto. I do some simple things when traveling to give me a little luck and a few "traveling mercies." Visualizing a safe arrival after an uneventful journey is the first thing I do. If I've been to the place before, I imagine myself there, with friends around me, greeting me with hugs and a cold drink. If the destination is new to me, I spend time looking at my feet and imagine them carrying me to my destination and being firmly on the ground, wherever that ground may be.

Having a travel talisman in your pocket or bag also makes good sense. I put a little piece of gravel from my driveway into my primary bag—which is usually my shoulder bag, the one that always stays with me. I speak these words to it before it goes in: "Don't worry, friend. I'll bring you back here, safe and sound. And I'll be with you the whole way."

My car has a good luck and safe travels talisman hanging from the turn signal post. It's a string of bright blue beads to ward off ill luck. You might also choose one of those blue and white "evil eye" beads, but my blue beads seem to do the trick.

Many non-Catholics have adopted Saint Christopher and his miraculous medal, which can be purchased in most church shops and online. He is known as the patron saint of travelers, but I prefer working with my own sacred ancestors and pass on the Saint Christopher medal. Try it if it appeals to you—it's pretty worn as a necklace or clipped to your car keys.

When driving, I pat the dashboard of my little red car—whose name is Vite-Vite—and say to myself, "Together safely and happily another 100,000 miles!" I do that when going on any long road trip and sometimes as an everyday blessing.

Protection

In chapter 8, we discussed protective magics as well as a few push-backs for those times when accountability is difficult to enforce. The following section offers a few templates for protecting yourself, the land with which you live, and those people you love.

Energy Clearing

We hear far too much about negative versus positive energy, and the drama that follows these declarations is largely unhelpful. There is a kind of paranoia that sets in when we think that people around us are somehow sending us bad energy in an attempt to hurt us or wreck our lives. I talked about this in the energy chapter, but I want to reenforce it here. When you are adept at shielding, little of this will get through, and if you spend a great deal of time fretting about this, you may not be as good at shielding as you think. Review your technique, and if you find it lacking, please choose another one to try.

The spaces in which you live and work can hold stagnant energy, however, and clearing that out can do wonders for your mood and ability to get things done. There are some standard ways to clear energy, but I find the best is to open all doors and windows and, using a broom, sweep through the place, getting into the corners, from front door to back, if you have one. Walk through the house making noise—I ring a cowbell but don't recommend quite that much noise if you live in an apartment building. You can utilize the same technique if you live in a room or a couple of rooms in a house where others live too. Afterward, close the windows and then the doors. Doing this once a moon cycle helps keep your space sweet and cuts down on dust bunnies too.

Seeing Better in Your Visualizations

As I've written before, I have weak vision that is corrected by eyeglasses. In the section on scrying, I related to you how I remove my glasses as a way to soften my vision for divination and trance. But sometimes I need to sharpen my vision and increase the clarity around any situation.

I have developed a meditation for this purpose. I make a cup of my preferred hot beverage and sit down in front of a lighted candle. I ground and breathe deeply. I watch the flame. There is not a push to clear my mind or to make it still; I merely drink my drink and watch the candle, letting my mind zip around. I recommend doing this for a week. It takes about eight minutes. For the first few days, your mind will continue to race and present thoughts and images. By the fourth day, all the zany stuff starts to sink to the bottom of your consciousness and there is a layer at the top that will focus your eye and your mind. Allow your mind to continue to work on those few things and make your intention to get the clarity required from this viewing. By the end of the week, you are likely to have a clear idea of what, if anything, you need to do or to say. It takes time but it is worth it.

Weather Work

Once upon a time, I was a wiz at weather work. When developing an outside event, I would tell the people organizing it not to worry about a backup location because the rain would hold off. And it did.

Here are some techniques you can try if you are interested in altering weather patterns. You may have a knack for this and it is a skill that is too often needed as climate shift accelerates. To do this work, I would first ground myself and face any visible clouds.

I raised my hand and did a shooing, get-away motion, saying, "Go away, away to the North! Go away, to where you are wanted!"

Likewise, I was good at bringing rain when the land was dry. Again, it began with a stout grounding. Then I imagined myself stretching up past the house and the trees and into the sky, where I would gather the small rain clouds and herd them into my area. Then I'd pat them gently to release the rain.

There is also a rain-calling working that involves half an eggshell in the nondominant hand. Into the eggshell goes some liquor, spit, and a bit of vervain. The thumb of the opposite hand goes into the center of the eggshell and winds the shell counterclockwise.

But I stopped weather magic a few years ago. The drought in the Southeast seemed as if it bore a lesson, wisdom to be learned about the land knowing what was needed better than I knew. I rarely interfere now, preferring to leave it to Mother Nature.

The Silver Thread

Here's the protocol for the Silver Thread or Silver Cord, which comes into Appalachian folk magic from its Irish roots. It is an old healing modality for connecting over a distance. It can be used for many purposes, but I have found it very effective for healing. Go to a place of meditation or into a relaxed but conscious awareness that is commonly called "alpha state" (because it increases the brain's alpha wave activity). Imagine the tips of the fingers of your dominant hand. Feel them warming up. Imagine that a white light forms at the tips and as it projects out into a beam or thread, it turns to silver. Then you imagine that thread leaving where you are and going directly to the person you are working for. Imagine it quite literally, as far as you can. It goes down the steps and out the front door and up the street and onto the highway and ... you get what I mean. When it arrives at its destination, send pulses of energy (always pulling the energy from the earth and not out of yourself) along the thread, breathing out healing, breathing in love. Break the connection by reeling the thread back in, like a fishing line. Finish by putting your hands together, pressing them into the earth, and coming back from your meditative state.

Candy Magic

One of the most popular classes I have ever taught is based on old-fashioned candies. I also wrote about candy magic in my book *Roots, Branches & Spirits*. Using these homely and inexpensive products is a gateway to the practices we've explored throughout this book. They illustrate the importance of practice and intention over ingredients and tools and offer a soft landing place for beginning spellcasters. It isn't about exotic or expensive ingredients but about your will and the stoutness of your practice.

No fancy jewelry required.

The Marshmallow Hex

This is the original working and is designed to take someone down to size. You need to gather up the biggest marshmallows you can find, a soft pencil, and some long thorns or toothpicks. First, write the name of the subject on the marshmallow as many times as will fit. Cover the entire surface. Then stick it with those thorns or toothpicks all over. Leave it outside for the ants and other insects to pick apart, bit by bit.

Necco Wafers, a.k.a. "Necro" Wafers

These can be used to bring your career, love life, or creativity back from the dead. Write the intention on the candy, wrap it in a paper sachet, and then bury it in a place you love and tend.

Reese's Cup Power Spell

These popular candies can be used to take away someone's power over you. You will need a Reese's Peanut Butter Cup and a sharp knife. Carve the name of the person on the top, then peel or cut it off and let it melt in your mouth. Do the same thing to the sides and peel them away and let them melt in your mouth. Do the same with the bottom of the candy. You may need to chill the peanut butter center to firm it up. Then roll it into a ball and pop it into your mouth. Done!

Jelly Beans for Your Heart's Desire

Jelly beans can be used as the magic beans from fairy tales that grow giant stalks. You can use them to achieve your heart's desire. Then bury them in the ground, three at a time, in a hill, like corn or cucumber seeds.

Other Old-Fashioned Candies to Consider

- *100s and 1000s or Candy Buttons:* To draw to you what you need
- *Atomic FireBalls:* To kick your new project into high gear
- *Bull's-Eye Caramels:* To be on target in that meeting or interview
- *Bonbons:* To call some leisure time your way

- *Chuckles:* To "cheer up" someone, either you or someone else; helping a sad sack see the bright side of life
- *Long Boys Coconut Caramels:* To promote sexual vigor
- *Mary Jane Taffy:* To help you set about improving your self-image, with the shiny new shoes these candies are named for
- *Rock Candy:* To be strong

Advanced Techniques

Here near the end of our time together—after we've spent so much time with simplicity and the craft of moving energy around—let's look at a couple of techniques that I consider advanced. Since we've explored the building blocks of practice, it seems only fair to outline a couple of tricky, fun, and practical protocols: glamoury and allure.

Glamoury

Glamoury, or casting a glamour, is such an old and practical magic that we mostly forget the magic part. We assume that those Hollywood stars and social media influencers simply have an extra helping of charm and an army of stylists to keep their look—their brand—on point. We use the word *glamour* to describe this razzle-dazzle.

Casting a glamour is a useful—and tricky—bit of magic that can be used to great advantage. The purpose of a glamour is to show the world (your intended audience) a façade over and around your body that allows you to be seen exactly as you wish to be seen. It's good for job interviews, court cases, and presentations for work. It takes a fair amount of energy to maintain and is raised in a similar manner to raising your personal shields.

As with much of the technique in this book, you will find ways that work more effectively for you, but here are the steps I use and the ones I teach.

Casting a Personal Glamour

Here are step-by-step instructions for glamour casting.

1. Determine what the purpose of the glamour is—promotion, success in speaking in public, and the like.

2. Stand in front of a portrait-size mirror. It is easier to focus on than a full-length one.

3. Ground in whichever way works best for you.

4. Draw in energy.

5. While looking into your own eyes, begin to build the image you require. For example, "I will be seen as skilled, confident, and respected and loved by my colleagues."

6. Start at the top of your head and with both hands move down the outline of your reflected silhouette.

7. Repeat the intention as your hands move, while looking into your reflected eyes. Move through this action (outlining your silhouette and repeating the intention) three times.

8. You may feel a sensation—cool for some, warm for others—that starts at your ankles and works its way up your body. It often centers on the face.

9. After the final pass, bring your hands down belly-high with palms upward, and press your fingernails into the palms of your hands until you feel the "bite." This sets the glamour.

You should monitor your energy throughout, making sure the working is powered. You may choose to also raise your shields. You can see how this requires consistent energy retrieval.

When you are ready to release the glamour, you can press your nails into your palms again, as you uncouple from your energy source. After the "bite," open your hands quickly and shake them out. Another way is to bring your hands up and around your reflected silhouette, doing the opposite gesture to the one you used to set the glamour. Do this three times, then release the glamour to the sky and wind. Uncouple from your energy source. In either case, you may find it good to eat some grounding food and drink some water to return fully to your embodied self. After you've taken care of that, check your grounding and go your ways.

Busting a Glamour

Removing another person's glamour can be helpful in inter-personal dealings. Most experienced magic-workers can detect a glamour and know when the user is taking unfair advantage. On the other hand, it can be gratifying to see someone presenting their very best selves (with just a touch of extra glow). Glamour, if used with good intent, can impart much needed self-confidence.

Here are the steps I use:

1. Ground yourself and start listening with your mind's ear.
2. Breathe deeply to clear your energy field.
3. Connect with your preferred energy source. This does not take the level of energy that is required for setting a glamour, oddly enough.

4. When you are ready to start, simply sit with your forearms resting on your thighs.

5. Open up your soft (nondominant) hand, palm-up, and begin tapping the center of that palm with the middle finger of your strong hand. You may start to feel one hand get warm and then the other.

6. When the energy feels to be flowing back and forth between the tapping hand and the receiving hand, look up at the person you believe is glamoured. Simply let your eyes rest upon them and keep tapping.

7. Soon you will be rewarded with seeing the person as they really are—tired, shaky, afraid, nervous. I give a little nod of thanks and keep tapping, to expose the glamour to the other people assembled.

8. Listen and feel the shifting of energies in the room.

9. Raise your personal shields.

10. When you have achieved the desired result, let your hands rest, palms down and facing the floor. You may also want to shake out your hands.

11. Check your grounding and your breathing.

12. Observe the changes in the subject.

This is a good example of the importance of strong shields during your own glamour-casting. If your subject seems to resist your glamour-busting, they may have excellent shields. Invite them for tea and ask how they do it.

Allure

This come-hither working is designed to invite people into the sphere of your influence, and it is achieved in a similar way as a glamour is. It is used—either consciously or subconsciously—by preachers, salespeople, and politicians.

Implemented to attract attention, as a glamour does, an allure has a further agenda: to draw the observer in, to "lure" them. It is attraction, with subsequent capture. You can see how that would be helpful for the sort of people listed above—see me, join me. Once you've gotten that attention, it will be up to you to use it wisely. Words to the wise: an allure is ineffective as a love charm, as it tends to encourage stalkers and other needy undesirables. There are certainly love charms that can be employed, but in my experience, they are dicey and tend to draw people you think you really, really want—who turn out to be really, really wrong for you. You usually end up having to pry them loose. Instead set your intention for the characteristics you look for in a partner, not for a specific person. That usually works much better, though the people who come to me looking for a magical answer to their loneliness never believe me.

One Scenario

You are a new teacher, fresh out of training. Your first job is in a system with a tough reputation. An allure will help get your students' attention and ease your transition into your chosen profession.

Here's how you might do that:

1. Work with a full-length mirror.
2. Review the steps for setting a glamour and enact them, ending with repeating the tracing of your silhouette three times.

3. Move your hands to your face, fingertips lightly touching your cheeks. Close your eyes, moving your fingertips to your eyes and touching your eyelids.

4. Bring your fingertips to your lips. Open your eyes, if you choose.

5. Fingertips now move to your throat, then to your heart.

6. Let your hands rise to the sides of your face and frame your reflected image.

7. Allow your hands to move down your silhouette to finish at your sides.

8. Slowly move your hands to cover your face, without touching, and then lower them below your chin.

9. Then place your hands crossed over your heart and let that gesture set the allure.

You can release the allure in the same way you release a glamour—by bringing your hands up and around your reflected silhouette three times. Release the allure, as with the glamour, to the sky and wind. Uncouple from your energy source. As before, you may find it good to eat some grounding food and drink some water to return fully to your embodied self, to ground yourself thoroughly.

Remember the Building Blocks

Are you feeling like a film star by now, with all this talk of glamour and allure? Practice these helpful techniques but don't overdo them. Most of us want a goal of being more authentic, not less. But every so often, we all need a little lift.

I trust that you understand that all the sample workings in this chapter are just that—templates to encourage you to practice and to become adept. Try them out, by all means, but we know the building blocks—the stepping stones—of effective magical practice lie in all those things we have practiced: setting a strong and clear intention, grounding, shielding, harvesting useable energy, and then sending it on its way.

Everything else, in the words of beloved author Terry Pratchett, is Boffo.[8]

❦

NOW YOU TRY

This chapter outlines some templates that can be used for your work. Remembering the techniques you've practiced so far will make the possibilities outlined here some fun exercises to test your skills.

Choose a working that tickles your fancy and practice it until you've made it your own. It is best to start with something that is useful in your day-to-day life. If you are a gardener, try bringing rain when needed. Your plants will thank you.

Hint: Remember to choose something simple and useful first.
It's so satisfying!

8. Terry Pratchett, *Wintersmith* (New York: HarperCollins, 2006), 10.

Conclusion
A Permission Slip You Don't Need

One day a week—when I am in town—I read tarot at our local metaphysical shop, Asheville Raven and Crone. There's a pretty and private reading room with a long table, and when I arrive, someone on staff hands me a schedule for the day. Sometimes it is back-to-back readings for four hours. Sometimes there's only one reading scheduled at the very end of the day. I take them as they come and read as best I can.

I've been reading cards for over half a century and began with playing cards, though now I use a tarot deck. As I've matured in my practice, I have found that much of what I do is a sort of counseling, advising people on the best things to do or the best way to be, given what the cards are indicating about the time in which they walk.

More and more people are floundering in these challenging times. They literally don't know what to do next. The world feels so different, so frightening, as if there is nothing that feels secure, nothing that can be trusted to be as it was even a few minutes before. When I ask them what their fervent desire is at that moment, they are often puzzled at the question because the life they lead doesn't allow for the "frivolity" of dreaming about what you want. They have been instructed through their personal histories and through family and church to limit the possibilities and get on with the work of life. Many people have been trained to not even question the way the world is but to accept it as the will of higher powers or as intractable situations over which they have no agency at all.

Another personal malady that inflicts itself upon the modern world is the insecurity many of us hold about our value in society. The constant judgmental drumbeat of the dominant culture would have us believe that we only truly have value when we abide by societal norms of conduct and dress. In addition to that, the lingering ghosts of our Puritan founders inflict on us the curse of busyness and tie our value into what we are able to produce and how hard we can work. Some of us feel that our sense of self-worth is directly tied to how much we get done in a day or a week or a lifetime. If we take time off for play or even for rest and healing, we know others will think less of us and judge us for our failure—because we have been seduced into judging ourselves when we can't meet impossible standards for production.

People do judge us. Social media is rife with it, and the overculture itself has come to a place where we are evaluated constantly and usually found wanting. The judgment is so heavy that it can seal us off from our creativity and dull our ears so that we don't hear all the good that is said because we are focused on the negative and the shaming that comes from that. When we hold ourselves against impossible standards—in any area—we are bound to be wanting, to be less than perfect and therefore unacceptable.

How did we get to this terrible place? We may have inherited the notion of achieving perfection from our parents' example of all work and no play. We may have received it from the religious institutions of our childhood and youth when we are raised in systems that hold us up to the perfection of a deity. It is usually understood that we are forgiven by the faraway deity for our missteps and misdeeds, but our human coreligionists are not required to do so and will hold us up as an example of how not to be. The show trials of Inquisitional Europe were designed to save souls (at the expense of destroying bodies) and to serve as a warning to anyone else who might be living in a state of nonconforming to community standards. It was—and is—a control mechanism to make sure the citizens know what is expected of them. Current standards are presented in the same way and require knowledge of what's au courant whether in fashion or opinion.

You have value simply by being. If you take nothing else away from this book on magical practice, I hope you will always remember that. Imposter syndrome may come to visit on occasion, but do not let it take up permanent residence in your soul or in your head. You do not have to calculate your value based on other people's expectations or by working so much that you never enjoy life.

The Land and the Body in Which We Dwell

In addition to all the witchery—or perhaps all the witchery is a result of it—I am an animist, someone who understands that everything we encounter in the natural world is ensouled. It colors all aspects of my life and of my magical practice. So when we consider the importance and the practice of grounding and earthing, knowing the land under our feet is both beneficial and I would say necessary.

In an earlier book, I repurposed the whole concept of coming into relationship with the land. I think we are already in that place and merely need to acknowledge the kinship, the profound connection. When we do that, the ability to ground into this beloved and known ecosystem all around us can be remarkably simple, an act we do every day without setting elaborate intention or complicated protocol. We do it because we cherish the relationship. We wake for another day of all that we do, and underlying all of it is this abiding bond of our physical selves and the body of the planet with which we dwell.

I teach classes that invite people to try all kinds of zany things, and most people join in the fun, getting the point of being in touch with our magical selves, our physical bodies, and our desires.

But some of my workshops are difficult for people to step into. One of them is a class on radical self-care and the other is based on my book *Embracing Willendorf: A Witch's Way of Loving Your Body to Health and Fitness*. In two workshops (one on radical care, another on loving our bodies), I ask the participants to set aside their self-loathing for their wonderful bodies and to take care of their own needs. I ask that they engage with their physicalities in ways they aren't often allowed. There is reluctance and there is also shame, as they replay old comments in their heads and review all the reasons they are not worthy of self-care and self-love.

All those situations bring us to the place where we begin to understand what we are up against when we're working to change the world for the better and to encourage people who claim to be magic folk to actually practice magic. That's when I pull out my invisible notepad and write out a permission slip.

It feels silly at first. I wiggle the closed fingers of my right hand across the open palm of my left hand, then mime ripping the sheet off and hand it to them. In the case of a class at one conference where I had suggested being kind to themselves and their communities, I stood up from my seat and walked to the door. I "nailed" the notepad to the side of the door and invited them to tear off a permission slip as they left the room. To my surprise and delight, several people did exactly that. One of them even folded the "paper" in half and stuck it in her purse.

The same people who will object to any sort of magic that affects someone as an abridgment of "free will" will happily assure us that we can always make our own reality, if only we are as deeply connected as they. And if we can't seem to move ourselves from toxic situations and people, those folks are happy to remind us (or bully us) to either "vibe higher" or focus our will. But society can be a brutal antagonist against which we have little real agency. Be patient with yourself as you go through the learning process of this or anything else. Create a helpful support network and do what you can do without comparison to others.

Failure as Growth

Sometimes you will fail. We all fail. We all try things that don't work, and it is not the time to give up in frustration. As with any new skill, step back from it and use your discernment to see if there was a piece missing or if you couldn't commit to the work for some reason. Maybe you were stressed because of home or work challenges. Maybe you had a headache coming on.

Anyone who tells you that their magic work never fails is either a liar or someone who doesn't do much magic. Failure is the only way I've learned to do all I do. Magic is a verb too. It is in the doing of it that we learn about the big pieces of the work as well as the subtleties. Your magic will change throughout your lifetime and observing the changes is always interesting.

The practices outlined in this book are exactly that. Practices. If you take nothing else away from these pages, I hope you will carry with you the idea that you will be most effective at this magic stuff if you practice it as often as possible. Don't "save" it until you need it. Do it now. Fling blessings throughout your day. Set an intention for the day as you fall asleep or as you make your breakfast tea. You will get better and better, and it will get easier and easier. The magic you practice as a person new to the whole shebang will be different from the magic you practice a year later. It will be vastly different ten years later. And, trust me, it will be far different fifty years later.

I want to remind you of the binding technique I wrote about earlier—the binding that involves a raw egg and string. You set your intention and write it on the shell of the egg with a pencil. When the shell is covered with your writing, you continue to repeat your intention as you wrap the egg in cotton thread, covering all the eggshell and writing. Tie the ends of the thread together and the working is set. Into the freezer it goes for a moon cycle.

As you become more versed in the feel of this sort of working, you will find shortcuts. At first, you'll set your intention. (You've learned that this part is vital, and if you're going to skimp on technique, this is not the place to do it.) Then you'll wrap the egg in a piece of soft paper, clutching it in your hand and setting the working. Other shortcuts will present themselves, and when you are adept, you will set the intention, tap your soft palm with the fingertips of your strong hand, and the working is set.

Simple. Elegant. Effective.

We use training wheels on bicycles for reasons of safety and to give us confidence as we are learning. Let all the steps of the workings you'll find in the back of this book assure you of the importance of process in the practice of magic. But don't feel that you must take every slow step after you've practiced your workings for a while. As with everything in magic, try out your shortcut and see if the final result meets your satisfaction. If it doesn't, go back to basics and see what you may have missed. Open yourself to beginner's mind.

Finally, it is indeed okay to do magic for yourself—to improve your health, your financial situation, your life in general. There is no shame in using all the tools in your workbasket to achieve what you need.

There's a funny meme called the "Ballard Query" that my friends created for me years ago because I am the nagging presence that often reminds people that there is work to do. It reads, "Ain't you people got no gods to worship? No holy days to celebrate? No ancestors to deal with—er, I mean, venerate? In short, don't you people have some sacred work to do? Justice work? Environmental work? Community weaving?"

Here, dear reader, is your permission slip to live an enchanted, magical life in a world that is endlessly and completely enchanted. No shame, no "Mundania." Only curiosity, success in your Work and life, and joy.

Go forth, my friend, and change the world.

Bibliography

Afanasyev, Alexander. *Vasilisa the Beautiful and Baba Yaga*. New York: The Planet, 2012.

Barker, Cicely Mary. *The Complete Books of the Flower Fairies*. London: Warne, 1996. Reprint, London: Penguin, 2002.

Bible. Authorized King James Version. Oxford University Press, 2008.

Black, George Fraser. *Scottish Charms and Talismans*. Edinburgh, UK: Neill and Company, 1894.

Cabot, Laurie. *Power of the Witch*, New York: Random House, 1990.

Child, Francis James, ed. *The English and Scottish Popular Ballads*. New York: Houghton, Mifflin and Company, 1904.

dePaola, Tomie. *Strega Nona*. Hoboken, NJ: Prentice Hall, 1975.

Eisler, Riane. *The Chalice and the Blade*. New York: HarperCollins, 1988.

Ehrenreich, Barbara. *Bright-Sided: How the Relentless Promotion of Positive Thinking Has Undermined America*. New York: Henry Holt, 2009.

Forbes, Bronwen. *Make Merry in Step and Song: A Seasonal Treasury of Music, Mummer's Plays & Celebrations in the English Folk Tradition*. Woodbury, MN: Llewellyn Publications, 2009.

Goldsmith, Barbara. *Other Powers: The Age of Suffrage, Spiritualism, and the Scandalous Victoria Woodhull*. New York: HarperPerennial, 1998.

Graham, Kenneth. *The Wind in the Willows*. New York: Penguin Classics, 2005.

Green, Marian. *A Witch Alone*. New York: Element, 2002.

Greene, Heather. *Lights, Camera, Witchcraft*. Woodbury, MN: Llewellyn Publications, 2021.

Homer. *The Odyssey*. Translated by E. V. Rieu and D. C. H. Rieu. New York: Penguin Classics, 2003.

Jacobs, William W. *The Monkey's Paw and Other Tales of Mystery*. Chicago: Academy Chicago Publishers, 1997.

Kellogg, Steven. *The Christmas Witch*. New York: Penguin, 1992.

King, Stephen. *Pet Sematary*. New York: Gallery Books, 2002.

Kimmerer, Robin Wall. *Braiding Sweetgrass: Indigenous Wisdom, Scientific Knowledge, and the Teaching of Plants*. Minneapolis: Milkweed Editions, 2013.

Latham-Jones, Cassandra. *The Village Witch: Life as a Village Wisewoman in the Wilds of West Cornwall*. Oxford, UK: Mandrake, 2013.

Leek, Sybil. *The Complete Book of Witchcraft*. New York: Penguin, 1973.

MacDonald, Glynn. *The Complete Illustrated Guide to Alexander Technique*. New York: HarperCollins, 1998.

Miller, Madeline. *Circe*. Boston: Little, Brown, 2020.

Ovid. *Metamorphoses*. Translated by David Raeburn. New York: Penguin Classics, 2004.

Polacco, Patricia. *Babushka Baba Yaga*. New York: Penguin, 1993.

Potter, Beatrix. *The Tailor of Gloucester*. London: Frederick Warne, 1902.

Pratchett, Terry. *Wintersmith*. New York: HarperCollins, 2006.

Rosas, Debbie, and Carlos Rosas. *The NIA Technique*. New York: Broadway Books, 2004.

Shakespeare, William. *A Midsummer Night's Dream: The Folger Shakespeare Library Edition*. New York: Simon and Schuster, 2004.

———. *The Tragedy of Hamlet, Prince of Denmark, Folger Shakespeare Library Edition*. New York: Simon and Schuster, 1992.

Simard, Suzanne. *Finding the Mother Tree: Discovering the Wisdom of the Forest*. New York: Knopf, 2021.

Stamets, Paul. *Mycelium Running: How Mushrooms Can Save the World*. New York: Ten Speed Press, 2005.

Watkins, Alfred. *The Old Straight Track*. Glastonbury, UK: The Lost Library, 2013.

To Write to the Author

If you wish to contact the author or would like more information about this book, please write to the author in care of Llewellyn Worldwide Ltd. and we will forward your request. Both the author and the publisher appreciate hearing from you and learning of your enjoyment of this book and how it has helped you. Llewellyn Worldwide Ltd. cannot guarantee that every letter written to the author can be answered, but all will be forwarded. Please write to:

H. Byron Ballard
℅ Llewellyn Worldwide
2143 Wooddale Drive
Woodbury, MN 55125-2989

Please enclose a self-addressed stamped envelope for reply, or $1.00 to cover costs. If outside the U.S.A., enclose an international postal reply coupon.

Many of Llewellyn's authors have websites with additional information and resources. For more information, please visit our website at http://www.llewellyn.com.